Rearing Children in a Postmodern World

By:

Carey N. Ingram

Copyright © 2022 **Carey Ingram Publishing**

All rights reserved. No part of this publication may be reproduced, distributed, or transmitted in any form or by any means, including photocopying, recording, or other electronic or mechanical methods, without the prior written permission of the publisher, except in the case of brief quotations embodied in critical reviews and certain other noncommercial uses permitted by copyright law. For permission requests, write to the publisher, addressed "Attention: Book Rights and Permission," at the address below.

Published in the United States of America

ISBN 978-1-959173-17-5 (SC)
ISBN 978-1-959173-87-8 (HC)

Carey Ingram Publishing
222 West 6th Street
Suite 400, San Pedro, CA, 90731
reving123@aol.com

Ordering Information and Rights Permission:

Quantity sales. Special discounts might be available on quantity purchases by corporations, associations, and others. For details, contact the publisher at the address above.

For Book Rights Adaptation and other Rights Permission. Call us at toll-free 1-888-945-8513 or send us an email at admin@stellarliteray.com.

Table of Contents

Foreword i
Special Thanks ii
Introduction iv
   Chapter 1 1
   Chapter 2 10
   Chapter 3 14
   Chapter 4 21
   Chapter 5 26
   Chapter 6 34
   Chapter 7 41
   Chapter 8 46
   Chapter 9 54
   Chapter 10 61
   Chapter 11 70
References 77

Foreword

On a daily basis, we observe children in our communities having to deal with hurt and pain in the home and at school. The African Proverb, "It takes a village to raise a child," is a true statement. However, the ultimate guidance for children living in the Postmodern Day World begins in the home. The church is the bridge that provides the religious support for leading families and children to Jesus Christ.

How can you nurture children in your church and lead them to Jesus Christ? A church must take steps to develop an effective children's ministry. It is important that an age-appropriate, interactive children's ministry exists in your place of worship.

The author, Carey N. Ingram, is a pastor and special education teacher who serves on the faculty of the National Baptist Congress of Christian Education. The course he teaches at the convention, "Ministering to Hurting Children," provides exemplary training for adults in the Children's Workers Division. I have known the author for many years, watching him grow up, his adult years as my pastor, and on the faculty at the convention. He not only has formal training as an educator and pastor, but he imparts knowledge from his experiences as a Christian family man in a Postmodern Day World.

This book is a "must read" for clergy, members of the congregation, and community who want to gain clear insight and direction in religious training for children and youth.

Proverbs 22:6: "Train up a child in the way he should go: and when he is old, he will not depart from it."

Esther Vaughn

Assistant Administrator, Department of Christian Education National Baptist Congress of Christian Education Auxiliary to the National Baptist Convention, USA,Inc.

Special Thanks

I am so blessed and I thank God for this opportunity to share my experiences and ideas by way of this book. That being said, I have to say, "Thank-You" to so many who in some way played a part in helping me with this project. First, and always, I am grateful for my dear wife Judy for her inspiration. She has been that mother, grandmother, youth director, surrogate mother, and social worker that I have observed for years patiently working with children and adolescents. Not just for her own family members, but whenever she sees a child in need, she reaches out to them. Thank you, Judy, for being a guiding light, a kind and gentle spirit who has always been there for your children and other children in their times of need. It is because of people like you that give me hope that we can make a difference in the lives of young people.

I want to recognize, honor, and give a special thanks to Dr. Nettie Wood, Administrator of the Youth Department of the Congress of Christian Education. Dr. Wood, I know that teaching the class, "Ministering to Hurting Children", was your special project. You gave birth to this class, and in a due season you entrusted your "baby" to me. Thank you for giving me an opportunity to share my views on this subject in that class for the last 9 years. You have been an awesome mentor. This book would not be possible without your having given me a chance to share your vision.

To my book team: First I am blessed to have a friend and wise counselor like Mrs. Laney Stevenson. Thank you Mrs. Stevenson for editing my book. Mrs. Linda Burse, Ms. Yatta Collins, Mrs. Esther Vaughn, Mrs. Carla Nation Freeman, Mrs. Tashia Twyman, Ms. Kelly Pugh, Mr. Curtis Adams, Miss Michelle Ingram, and Ms. Charlene Ransby, thank-you for your book cover ideas, advice, and promotions. Last, but not least, I give a "Shout Out" to my Lovejoy Church Family and the Pastor's Aid Ministry for giving me the support and encouragement that "I can do all things through Christ who strengthens me". I am blessed to be surrounded by family and friends who freely share their gifts and talents for causes bigger than all of us.

Finally, I dedicate this book to every parent who would read this material and others like this to give themselves a chance to be the best parent they can be. Children are a gift from God. What we do with them is our gift to God.

Introduction

At the time of this publication, I have been an instructor in the National Baptist Congress of Christian Education, which is the Youth and Adult Education branch of the National Baptist Convention, USA, Inc. For almost a decade, I have taught the class entitled, "Ministering To Hurting Children." From this class has come a tremendous learning experience for me. The most important thing I have come to realize is that our children, regardless of their socio-economic or education background, need positive reinforcement and encouragement from parents and guardians. Their ability to grow and mature to be happy, successful, and responsible citizens depends on continual nurturing from parents and everyone in the community of the family from the big sister or brother, barber, cosmetologist, pastor, Sunday School Teacher, classroom teacher, coach, or next door neighbors. Let the word go forth: "It does take a village to raise a child." This idea must be shared with all, and we all must be held accountable to rise to the occasion of being positive role models for children whenever and wherever we see them.

It appears we have lost a few generations of people to a lifestyle whose end result is detrimental and destructive. Generations of young people have had to plot their own course. Without any support and history to reflect upon, they have created their own. Some have done well, but most have succumbed to lifestyles void of morals, education and marriage. Generations have had to settle for minimal pay wage jobs or no job, single parent lifestyles, crime, and prisons.

Now, this book is not about casting the blame, judging, or condemning any particular culture that I personally do not agree with or fully understand. Rap music, Hip Hop Culture, drug culture, or alternative lifestyles are the result of a changing world. I suggest that the greater problems rest in the fact that when African Americans began to redefine themselves after the Civil Rights Movement, we failed to secure the family unit, despite all the progress made. Yes, I am saying we became selfish with a mentality that said, "I've got mine; you get yours." There seemed to be a "church on every corner." However, many people who needed the church to learn those church values were overlooked and not evangelized. In fact, some church members did not want certain types of people in their churches. Imagine that. Integration of school meant we all got brand new books, but we also got predominantly white teachers who did not know our culture well enough to reach our children. Therefore, they could not teach them or did not care enough to reach them to teach them. The drop-out rate continues to climb, however, I do not blame the teachers totally. At the end of the day, it is the parents' responsibility. Those who bring children into this world must ensure their overall well being. Parents must teach the basics and work together in the neighborhood along with the church, school, and civic organizations to form that village that will help rear that child.

You may say, " I live in a diverse neighborhood and they are not friendly. My church is located on the other side of town. Our children have friends who do not live in our neighborhood; therefore, it is hard to form a relationship that is impressionable for the lessons we want to teach and share." My question is, "Where is the village?" Well, it is there. You simply have to diligently work to bring it together. You must be the catalyst that makes your neighborhood friendlier and more environmentally safe, or you must move. You can no longer be a pew member of your church; rather, it is time to be a willing worker in your church. Seek God; see the need; then fill the void. There are many just like you in church with children looking for ways to help them grow.

The purpose of this book is to give hope to those who are overwhelmed by the worldly conditions around them. Here we are in a world where technology constantly changes the way we live. Parents and children can work these gadgets but seem unable to communicate with each other. From our neighbors next door to disasters across the world, how do I prepare my children to live in an ever changing and unpredictable world? Many wonder, "How can I keep my children safe, stable, and happy in the midst of my career or lack thereof ?" Here we are now in the postmodern day world which is full of temptations that could change our lives forever. How do we teach our children to be on guard and yield not to those temptations that could destroy their hopes, dreams, and ultimately their lives? How do we teach them to live a life that is pleasing in the eyes of the true and living God in this postmodern day world?

I do not have all the answers, but I do have some basic ideas and suggestions to share. In my years of experience as a parent, teacher, pastor, mentor, and observer of children, I am optimistic to share with you that it is possible to successfully rear your children in this ever changing world. Remember, as the world is forever changing, God never changes. The Master of the Universe has given us some basic rules, core values, and standards that have stood the test of time. Come with me on my journey and let me share my optimistic views with you.

Chapter 1

Understanding and Living In A Postmodern World

THE PROBLEM DEFINED

I do not believe anyone will argue that for as good as our children have it in this country, they also face obstacles, lifestyle challenges, and other issues that were less frequent or nonexistent for those of us born before 1964. Today's youth live in a time of high technology with computers, high definition television, iPhones, iPods, and iPads, to name a few. All of these are a part of the home, school, church, and recreation areas. However, when it comes to defining a hurting child in today's society, the list is inexhaustible, but some problems are more obvious. I am definitely saying that we had a better childhood than children have today. Life was so much simpler and innocent. That is not to say that it was perfect, but it was better. I want to suggest that every child is a hurting child to some degree. I say that because of the unexpected things children face daily. For example, the Hurricane Katrina Disaster, the Haiti Earthquake, and the recent earthquake and subsequent tsunami wave in Japan affected the children directly involved, but they also affected children everywhere who watched the plight of these areas over a period of time. Let's face it, we are seeing tremendous disasters on a regular basis and they are affecting all of us. "Therefore shall his calamity come suddenly; suddenly shall he be broken without remedy" (Proverbs *6-15).* Has the world become that wicked person that now must reap what has been sowed? What price do our children have to pay? The 911 terror attack, wars and upheavals in many countries, and natural disasters in recent years have had profound effects on our children's psyches. The end result is children from all backgrounds are not feeling safe. They may not say it or express it, but in time, we will see the result of children not feeling safe.

Who is the hurting child? To further examine this idea, here is a list of what children and teenagers face everyday:

- Temptations of drugs and alcohol
- Tremendous pressure to have sex and challenges about their sexuality (heterosexual, bisexual, and/or homosexual)
- Greater pressure on all age students to compete and succeed in school
- Loneliness and depression
- Fear of the police (some respect the law and stay out of jail while others have total disregard for the law and see the police as the enemy)
- Everyday threats of being kidnapped or at worst, gunned down in some areas
- Challenges to live for Christ in an ungodly society
- Sexual exploitation (even slave trade in some countries) by an adult (male or female)
- Concerns about staying healthy and not being obese
- Peer pressure
- The puberty crisis of feeling unattractive and inadequate
- Worries about wars and terrorism which result in being separated from family members involved in wars for periods of time per year
- Concerns about having money to have fun like their peers
- Concerns about how mama and daddy are doing

Our children are often labeled and must live with that label for the rest of their lives. They are labeled Autistic, Attention Deficit Hyperactivity Disorder, Emotionally Disturbed, Learning Disabled, or Physically Disabled. I am not saying the diagnosis is not true, but when you label a child, it tends to put him in a category where he often has no support and, therefore, has no hope of getting to that place we call "normal." The question is, "What has brought us to this point?" Let me share my theory with you.

A POSTMODERN WORLD

This idea of a Postmodern World first came to my attention more than a decade ago when our church family shared in sponsoring a Men's workshop with the Rev. C.L. Jordan, who, at the time, was the Pastor of a church in Cartersville, Georgia. We were privileged to have Dr. Larry Mercer, formerly of Moody Bible Institute and presently President of Washington Bible College in Washington D.C.

Dr. Mercer taught a Parenting Class and brought to light some things that many people still had not grasped or perhaps did not even have a clue about, and it is this: It is a different world today from the world we came from. In today's society, we have two worlds: the Modern world and the Postmodern world. Unfortunately, these two worlds are different in attitudes, trains of thought, behaviors, and ideas as to what is valued in life.

My own fascination about this subject led me to discover that the modern world (the Baby Boomer's Generation and before) are those people born before 1964. We are rooted and grounded in what our parents taught us. We know what we believe to be right and wrong. Our core values are Bible based. We trust the Bible. The Bible is absolute truth. Consider this scripture: "For we wrestle not against flesh and blood, but against principalities, against powers, against the rulers of the darkness of this world, against spiritual wickedness in high places" (Ephesians 6:12). Therefore, in the modern world, the enemy is clearly defined. Now, this is not to say that we do exactly what we know to be right every time, but we do know that our enemy for life is a fallen angel, a spirit being whose name is Satan. Satan, or the devil, has a legion of spirit beings that follow him called demons. They are out to destroy the work of God and God's people on the earth. In fact, we believe that the word of God, the Bible, is inerrant and infallible. Again, we never measure up to it, and we certainly misinterpret it at times, but we know, as Christians, that with the aid of the Holy Spirit, that truth is brought to light in the word of God. It alone can guide us through this world and back to our Heavenly Father.

Another example of modern world thinking is that for the Christians, we believe Jesus is the only Savior of the world. Jesus the Christ is the anointed Messiah and only through belief in Him can we obtain eternal life. The scripture declares, "Jesus is the way, the truth, and the life: no man cometh unto the Father, but by me" (John 14:6). Further, for those my age and older, it is settled that marriage is defined as a man and woman joined in holy matrimony. We believe that divorce is what God allows but not what he intended. We believe that in the preeminence of love: "Though I speak with the tongues of men and of angels, and have not charity, I am become as sounding brass, or a tinkling cymbal… Charity suffered long, and is kind; charity envied not; charity vaunted not itself, is not puffed up, Doth not behave itself unseemly, seeked not her own, is not easily provoked, thinketh no evil; Rejoiced not in iniquity, but rejoiced in the truth; Beareth all things, believed all things, hoped all things, endured all things. Charity never failed… where everything else may fail, love will always bring the crown of life which is life abundant, and life everlasting" (1 Corinthians 13:1 ;4-8). As Christians, we believe love to be the guiding force in our lives.

However, the thinking is not the same in what is called the Postmodern World, which refers to those born after 1964. Also called Generation X and the 13th Generation, these groups initially defined themselves with the train of thought that you can fear it or face it. The year 2002 began the Internet Generation.

In the Postmodern World, reality is what you create it to be. There are no absolutes. Everything is based on relativism. We see this in the media. Art once imitated life; now life imitates art. The Postmodern World lives life based on feelings. They reject absolute truths. Believe it or not, the Bible tells us that such generations of people would come. This is not to say that everyone in recent generations thinks this way, just like everyone born before them do not fully embrace the Bible. But, generally speaking, far too many of the latter generations reject the Bible, and therefore, they reject God as absolute truth.

This is first pointed out in the Old Testament: "He is the Rock, his work is perfect: for all his ways are judgment: a God of truth and without iniquity, just and right is he. They have corrupted themselves; their spot is not the spot of his children: they are a perverse and crooked generation" (Deuteronomy *32:4-5)*. Hear Jesus' description: "And the lord commended the unjust steward, because he had done wisely: for the children of this world are in their generation wiser than the children of light" (Luke 16:8).

All these scriptures point us to the Jewish Race, God's people, who rejected Jesus Christ as Lord and Savior. Paul spoke of his people in this manner: "And with many other words did he testify and exhort, saying, Save yourselves from this untoward generation" (Acts 2:40). Could it be that as time passes, every new generation is growing farther away from God?

So, the Postmodern World stands in contrast to the modern world. For example, sex before marriage is most acceptable in this untoward generation. In the beginning, marriage was between a man and woman, but today, it could also be between a man and man or woman and a woman. A CNN News Poll in early 2011 reported that 40% of Americans under the age of 30 saw marriage as obsolete. From my own experience, I have observed many couples content living together and not getting married at all. There is a present trend where women want and have children without a husband in the relationship. A woman just needs a sperm donor. Ideas such as these and others suggest God is just a matter of individual opinion. You have a God; I have a God. There is no right, no wrong, and no sin. There is even a train of thought that says there is no hell, and that all creation will go to heaven.

Now, here is the challenge to the Christian family. First, we live in a society that clearly rejects Biblical authority, including the Jewish Nation's rejection of Christ, Scientology, or someone as powerful as Oprah Winfrey, who has used her influence to suggest to people that Jesus may not be the only way of Salvation (therefore to Heaven), and the list goes on and on. You have websites that invite you to sign up to denounce the Holy Spirit in your life. To a Christian, that is blasphemy.

Second, there is a reluctance to submit to authority figures: parents, police, pastors, teachers, and others in leadership positions. These individuals are not respected for who they are in trying to guide people.

Third, there is the denial of absolute truths. To many, the Bible is now a book not to be reverenced and believed; rather, it is a book of myths and stories that may or may not be true.

Fourth, Satan is challenging anyone who will listen to those things that were once conceded to be right.

Consider these terms with which we need to re-familiarize ourselves in facing family issues:

1. Know that immorality is that which is ungodly and wrong, conflicting with generally or traditionally held moral principles.
2. Morals are practices or teachings: modes of conduct, a standard of our ethics and morale.
3. Amoral is neither moral nor immoral (good or bad) until you make the decision as what to do with a component that carries it.

For example, the media, music, TV, computer, cell phones, and other objects or trains of thought are harmless in and of themselves. These amoral things are neither good nor bad until they get into a person's hand or mind; then it depends upon what a person does with them.

What must we do? Let me say that now is not the time for Christian neutrality in this Postmodern Society. Now is the time for us to act. Our greatest resource, our youth, is at risk. We cannot afford to pretend all is well when there are so many hurting children in almost every facet of life. Children with no direction are doomed.

There is a story of an old lady who had a farm. One day, as she stepped out the back door to go into her garden, a frog at her door jumped into the house. It went straight to the kitchen where it hopped up on a kitchen chair and onto the kitchen table. His curiosity moved him to jump another level up to the kitchen stove. On top of the stove, he sensed water and jumped into a kettle filled with it. There, the frog decided to relax a minute and enjoy his new environment. Unknown to him, the old lady had turn on the stove to heat the water for vegetables she had gone to the garden to retrieve. The frog continued to enjoy the water but noticed that it was getting warm. This was a totally new environment to him, and he had no clue as to the impending danger. So, even as it got hotter and hotter, he continued to relax in the water. Then, the frog thought, "This heat will surely decrease." He remained in the hot kettle of water where he was beginning to sweat. Then, at that very moment, he thought to hop out of the water. The old lady brought mixed vegetables and put them in the pot. Now, the frog was content to rest on a green leaf and nibble off pieces of the other leaves. The frog was on what he assumed to be a lily pad while he enjoyed a snack. However, by this time, the water was almost to a boiling point, and the frog realized he was in a world of trouble. Unfortunately , when he went to hop out of the water, he found out he had no strength and his feet had swollen to the point he could not hop at all. Therein was the demise of this healthy but unwise frog. The point: this is a situation in which too many of our youth find themselves. A curious, innocent walk in the wrong direction, and one could end up in a fight, sometimes a fight that could costs them their lives. Young people are often seduced into situations and places where all seems good and comforting, only to find out later that it is slowly destroying the very fibers of their lives. What is our resolve in holding our family together in this Postmodern Day World?

I contend that we must declare war and remember God cannot use cowardly soldiers. This is warfare. We must fight for the hearts, souls, and minds of our children. Satan says, "You can have the children on Sunday; just give them to me the other six days." He knows the values displayed at most schools and on television, in general and specifically, on MTV, TH1, and BET, who have little or no redeeming value toward God. Therefore, parents must play a greater role in the lives of their children. This is one of the most awesome scriptures in the Bible that details parents' responsibility to their children: "And thou shalt love the LORD thy God with all thine heart, and with all thy soul, and with all thy might. And these words, which I command thee this day, shall be in thine heart: And thou shalt teach them diligently unto thy children, and shalt talk of them when thou sittest in thine house, and when thou walkest by the way, and when thou liest down, and when thou risest up (Deuteronomy 65-7).

POSSIBLE SOULUTIONS

How do we begin to address the problem in your home to counter the ungodly world that we face each day. "Ministering to Hurting Children" is a possible solution, and perhaps we can start with the following suggestions:

1. Make sure your home is a spiritually wholesome, safe and sacred haven. In a song I heard, "A house is not a home until there is love in the house." God is creator, sustainer, and the source of power. He is love. God wants center stage in our homes. Does God have center stage in your home? My wife has a theme for just about every room in our house. Our den area is "the zoo." She has statues of elephants, bears, zebras, ducks, and the list goes on. It creates an atmosphere of playfulness for my grandchildren and me. It is a place where we naturally congregate, relax and have fun. We may or may not turn on the TV. We can generally make our own fun with games, talking, and singing songs. However, in the foyer and the living room area is an entirely different story. When you enter the front door of our home, you'll see two beautifully framed messages. One says, "Welcome to the Power House of Carey and Judy Ingram where we honor the Lord, and He honors us with His presence." The other picture shares the 12 Old Testament names of God. This picture was given to us by dear friends. On a small table in the foyer are pictures of my wife and me when we were first married and pictures that celebrate our 25th Anniversary of marriage.

The living room has a more traditional look. We have one cabinet with all of our honors, trinkets, and other keepsakes, and yes, the Holy Bible sits open on the coffee table. A family portrait adorns our front wall. Without effort, the living room is definitely a special and sacred space. Sometimes, we entertain company in this room. But more often than not, we spend time praying in this room. It is a special and quiet place. I want to believe that everyone who comes through my front door feels and comes to know that they are in a special place.

Throughout the rest of the house, my wife has devotionals and all sorts of Christian literature so displayed that you feel welcome to pick it up. In other words, when you come in my home, I am confident that you feel you're in a special place. You immediately know what we stand for. The scenery, the literature, and the spirit of the home all point you to Christ. The conversation, if not initially, will soon be about the goodness of God. My point is you must create an environment and atmosphere in your home that helps and heals the wounded spirit. Encouragement and confidence should manifest itself in our homes. Have the kind of home that allows you to build up the character of those who come to your home. If you have Godly character, build your personal character into the lives of your family and those who come to your home. I am convinced that people, in general, (especially your children and grandchildren) are naturally drawn to the love of God that dwells within you.

2. Capture life's teaching moments. Do not miss the moment. Take advantage of the daily news, current events, and things around you to point your family to Christ. Do not be passive or aggressive, but rather, be assertive. Be sensitive to the Holy Spirit's voice. Timing is important. What you say and how you present it is important. Know that the salvation of a soul is at stake. You could be a part of changing someone's life forever.

It is amazing how what you read in the paper or the news reported on television or radio (whether good news or bad news) can be your opportunity to point someone (especially a child or teenager) to Christ and to positive moral living. An example is Tuesday, January 12, 2010, the day of the earthquake in Haiti, which left the capital city of Port-Au-Prince in ruins. I remember how the Lord placed it on my heart to pray for that country with the youth of our church at the Wednesday night Bible Study. After I prayed, I reminded them to just think how it would be, what they would do, and how they would feel if we had suffered such an earthquake. I reminded them of just how blessed we are and not to take it for granted. Then, I asked what was it that we could do to help the people in need. We prayed again and decided that we would raise some money to send to help the recovery effort in that area. The earthquake in Haiti was a great opportunity for me to witness to our young people about God. Why would He allow something like that to happen? What is His response? What is our response? What is God saying to the rest of the world? That is what I call a life teaching moment.

As Christian parents of teens, we must recognize the times in which we live and do the one most important and effective thing for our world, our country, our community, and our home: "Be an example of a believer." If we do that, we can be positive contributors and help make a difference in what is called the Postmodern Day World.

Chapter 2

The Origin of the Dysfunctional Family and How We Got Here

While man is attempting to alter God's design and Satan seeks to entirely destroy it, the family was and remains the first and greatest institution known to man. Biblically, the family begins with the single unit of one man and one woman. "Therefore a man leaves his father and his mother and clings to his wife, and they become one flesh" (Genesis 2:24). This is clear evidence that we are all included in the definition of family. Amid all the varieties found across cultural and color lines, researchers of modern science lead to a conclusion fully accordant with our sacred history that we are all of one species and of one family. "And hath made of one blood all nations of men for to dwell on all the face of the earth, and hath determined the times before appointed, and the bounds of their habitation" (Acts 17:26). Therefore, regardless of the good, bad, ugly, race, creed, color or nationality, we are all brothers and sisters of the family we call the human race.

Christ defines marriage also in Matthew *19:4-5,* He combined quotations from Genesis 1 and Genesis 2. He declared: "He who made them from the beginning made them male and female (1:26), and said, For this cause shall a man leave his father and mother, and shall cleave to his wife; and the two shall become one flesh (2:24). This means marriage and family are mentioned in the opening chapters of the Old and New Testaments.

Look at the wonderful institution of marriage as God ordained it. Here was Man and woman (woman literally means "Man with a womb"). God allowed him to name his wife Eve which means life giver, the mother of all living things. So they were in the image of God: knowledgeable, righteous, holy, and innocent before God. All was well until, in layman's terms, "somebody came creeping into the house." The state of the dysfunctional family all started with Adam and Eve. Their disobedience towards God now causes man to labor in the fields and woman to have pains during birth. We can also take a look at their descendants, Cain and Abel. Due to jealousy and hatred, one brother takes the life of the other. These are just two classic examples of how the first family was also dysfunctional. The Wikipedia Web dictionary defines a dysfunctional family as a family in which conflict, misbehavior and even abuse on the part of individual members of the family occur continually leading other members to accommodate such actions. This being the case, I think all families are dysfunctional at some point and time.

Now, the obvious question is how did we come to be dysfunctional, and how can we regroup and be the family God would have us to be? Well, I suggest most all of our troubles are a result of sin. Sin, in layman's terms, is simply, "missing the mark." It is any transgression against God, whether by committing or omitting some act. The first sin was born out of pride by an Angel named Lucifer when he decided it was he, and not God, who was shining bright in Heaven. Can you imagine the creature thinking more of himself than he thought of the Creator? "Thou art the anointed cherub that covered; and I have set thee so: thou was upon the holy mountain of God; thou hast walked up and down in the midst of the stones of fire. Thou was perfect in thy ways from the day that thou was created, till iniquity was found in thee" (Ezekiel 28:14). That same Lucifer transformed himself into a serpent and seduced Eve to bite from the tree of the knowledge of good and evil. Likewise, Eve seduced her husband. This disobedient act brought sin into the world and the family. We have been proned to be dysfunctional ever since. When Adam and Eve had children, iniquity and sin became a part of their nature.

Genesis 3 shows how sin disrupts relations between God and human beings and between man and wife. Additionally, Genesis 4 shows it destroying the bonds of brotherhood. Indeed, Cain is portrayed as a more hardened sinner than Adam. Although killing one's brother is more wicked than eating a protected fruit, both men committed sin against God. Adam was persuaded to sin, and Cain could not be dissuaded from sinning, even by God himself (Genesis 4:6-7). Sin is personified as an animal waiting to pounce (see 1 Pet. *5:8)*. When questioned by God about his sin, Adam, thought rather petulant, at least told the truth; Cain lied and then made a joke about it (Genesis 3:9-11; 4:9). Adam accepted God's judgment in silence, but Cain protested fiercely (Genesis 4:13-14) and was dispatched even further from Eden.

So what happened to the first family? We briefly see so much good; yet, we see evil as well. We see love, yet there is hatred. We see pride as they seek to be like God; yet, humility is seen in Adam when his punishment is decreed. We see the first religious act when Abel and Cain offer sacrifices unto the Lord. One sacrifice is accepted; another is not. Sadly, within the first family is also the first murder. There are four people on the earth and one brother murders the other because of jealousy, envy, and pride. When God punishes Cain with a curse that the ground would not support him, meaning as a farmer his seeds would never grow, Cain thought it was too harsh. God marked him signifying to all that if you confront Cain, God would confront you in a worst way.

Through the examples set by the first family, I can conclude that the first family represents the best and the worst of families of today. Since family is considered an individual unit and the whole human race, within lies our love and devotion towards each other, and we cannot disregard our faults and failures. What can the family do to get on and stay on the right path with God? Every family ought to pray. For I heard it said and I agree that 'a family that prays together stays together.' Adam and Eve were banished from the Garden of Eden. They had to leave paradise. Cain was cursed for the rest of his life, but the good news is that in spite of themselves, God never stopped loving them. This is the family's hope and herein is our victory. No matter the circumstance, even when doing wrong and coming short of the glory of God, God loves his families. He hates sin, but He loves the sinner. And I can hear Jeremiah saying, "Thus saith the LORD the maker thereof, the LORD that formed it, to establish it; the LORD is his name; Call unto me, and I will answer thee, and shew thee great and mighty things, which thou knowest not" (Jeremiah 33:1-3). Pray early in the morning at the rising of the sun. Pray when the sun is standing at high noon, then late in the mid-night hour, keep on praying. Paul says, "Pray continually, and pray without ceasing."

My first challenge to every man with a family is to pray daily with them. Start your day with a time of meditation and prayer designed by you. It does not have to be anything pious, religious, or boring. However, it should be sincere and from your heart, straight from the heart of God. Remember, your first obligation to your family is to secure their spiritual well-being. If you are not present in your home, a daily phone call to your children is better than nothing at all. Start somewhere and let it grow into what God would have it become.

If there is no father around, then it becomes the obligation of the mother to daily invoke the presence of God into her family through prayer. Perhaps in time, it can be a shared responsibility with the children. It can be a wholesome, challenging, yet endearing way to start your day with God. Once everyone is accustomed to practicing praying, each person can add to this devotional period. This will add yet another blessing to your family. Prayer eventually becomes a part of your life and it can only bless you. If you remember nothing else I've stated in this chapter, remember that 'A family that prays together stays together.'

Chapter 3

To Discipline or Punish Our Children…Which?

I am a certified teacher of the program, "Nurturing God's Way." This is a program that takes a holistic approach in nurturing families so that all family members are ministered to at the same time within their age group. That is to say that all the parents share a class, and all the teenagers share a class, etc. Babysitters are provided so there is no excuse for not attending the program. This program is offered once a week in the evenings, and dinner is also provided on that night.

One of the components of the 21 week course deals with the question of "Discipline As Opposed to Punishing a Child." I shall always remember my first training for this program and the day we got to the topic of punishing a child. When the instructor finished her presentation, she made it clear that we should consider moving away from the idea of spanking a child. I recall how adamantly opposed I was to such an idea! My mother had spanked me, whipped me, and when I was older, struck me with whatever was available and I turned out to be just fine. At the time, I had no scripture to back my train of thought except, "If you spare the rod, you spoil the child."

I'm glad I had the kind of instructor who was patient with me. In the end, she made it clear that I could hold fast to my personal belief but to make sure I gave parents I taught the option of not spanking their children and finding alternative means to redirect their child's misbehavior. I thought about that for days, and days turned into weeks until one day when it became clear to me that though my mother had been one to punish me severely when she deemed it necessary, I was also aware that I had rarely spanked my own children. Therefore, when I began to teach the class, I had come to a great compromise: Spanking or hitting a child as punishment should be only at certain times and/or in crucial situations.

Punishment and discipline are both methods for redirecting behavior. Punishment is a form of suffering, inflicting pain or loss that serves as retribution. It can be a penalty inflicted through the courts. Discipline is so much more than punishment. In fact, punishment is one form of discipline. Discipline is also giving instructions; it is a field of study. Discipline is training that corrects, molds, or perfects the mental faculties or moral character. Discipline is control gained by enforcing obedience or order. It is a pattern of behavior, and the end result is self control.

Now, an obvious question is when (or is it appropriate) to punish (inflict pain) on a child? In other words, is it still appropriate to use a rod, switch, paddle, or your hand to spank a child? The Old Testament makes it clear that the rod is definitely an instrument for punishing a child. What is a rod? The Hebrew meaning is: shebet, shay'bet; a scion, i.e. (literally) a stick (for punishing, writing, fighting, ruling, and walking, etc). Observe the Old Testament scripture and the manner in which it speaks of the use of a rod. "Wisdom is found on the lips of him who has understanding, But a rod *is* for the back of him who is devoid of understanding" (Proverbs 10:13 (NKJV). "He who spares his rod hates his son, But he who loves him disciplines him promptly" Proverbs 13:24 (NKJV). "Foolishness *is* bound up in the heart of a child; the rod of correction will drive it far from him" Proverbs 22:15 (NKJV). "The rod and rebuke give wisdom, but a child left *to himself* brings shame to his mother" (Proverbs *29:15* (NKJV).

When I was growing up, "Spare the rod and spoil the child" was a common saying for my parents. However, we should remember that Proverbs does not recommend brutal beatings, nor is physical chastisement the only instrument of child training mentioned. Indeed, instruction in righteousness and in the fear of the Lord is that without which mere whipping will fail. Question: When does this form of discipline that we call punishment become detrimental? Keep in your mind the idea of discipline and that punishment is just one way to discipline a child. For example, let me share another Old Testament scripture that points us to disciplining a child without laying a hand or instrument on the child. "Train up a child in the way he should go, And when he is old he will not depart from it" (Proverbs 22:6 (NKJV). Train up a child. This is not a common word for "educate," but the meaning is clear and the promise is a rich one. I am in no way suggesting that we not adhere to the Bible and the idea of the use of the rod as mentioned in the Old Testament. However, I do want to place emphasis on the fact that I believe the use of the rod (or punishment) to inflict pain for restitution and /or to teach a lesson should be done with precise timing. I get the impression that the use of a rod referred to in the Old Testament was for that adolescent (almost grown man) who simply would not be controlled. If this young teen had broken a law that he knew was wrong, (stealing, sexual assault, battery, or some other ungodly act and sin) a rod on his back seemed most appropriate. He was not old enough for prison, but yet punishment of some sort was in order. Then, the most humane of all punishment was, perhaps, the use of the rod. Yes, the rod had its place then and it has its place now. Again, I suggest timing is most important. For example, to beat a child with a rod, switch, stick, belt or hand is against the law in many states. I also suggest that hitting a child past the age of six for any reason can do more harm than good. Today, inappropriately striking, hitting, or spanking a child can result in: 1. Teaching your children that they can control others by using intimidation and physical force; 2. Discouraging your children from solving conflicts by reasoning and negotiating; 3. Increasing the chance that your children may be abusive to their children; 4. Making it more likely that your children will become rebellious toward you when they reach adolescence; 5. Making it less likely that your children will develop sensitivity to the feelings of others, and 6. Seriously harming your children and possibly ending up in the courts.

I strongly suggest that spanking, paddling, or whipping a child should be an exception, and not the rule. Let me give you a couple of examples of the exception. A few years ago, when my granddaughter, Lauren, was only three years old, she gave us the scare of our lives. We had just finished enjoying a wonderful Thanksgiving Dinner at my home. The house was full of family, and we had enjoyed a delicious dinner and were laid back watching television or chatting around the house. Normally, it is only my wife and me at our home. Perhaps, this is why she failed to put out a scented candle that was lit in the restroom. It was sitting on a counter in a corner well out of the way of most everything.

Lauren went to use the restroom. However, when she was washing her hands, apparently she noticed that the candle was lit. Lauren is smart and knows about the danger of fire, but her curiosity got the best of her that day. After washing her hands, she took a paper towel and placed it on the candle. Naturally, the paper towel ignited. When this happened, Lauren immediately took the burning paper and put it in the toilet where the flames were doused by the water. All of this happened in a matter of seconds, and the smell of burning paper towel immediately went all over the house. As Lauren ran out of the bathroom, she was met by her grandmother. As her grandmother began to put this puzzle of what happened together, Lauren's mother came in and with one look of Lauren's face, she knew exactly what had happened. Within a matter of seconds, Lauren confessed to her mom what she had done. Her mother immediately took her in a nearby bedroom and spanked her. It was about five hard hand licks on Lauren's bottom. It was a matter of serious injury, house on fire, or even death, and her mother treated it as such. She wanted Lauren to feel the potential of what she might have brought on herself, the pain of fire on the body. It was painful and hurtful, and it sent a great signal to Lauren to stay away from and not to play with fire. Lauren cried, but no one was permitted to comfort her. She was left alone in the room for about five minutes at which time her mother went in and explained why she had spanked her (I do not think she had spanked her before). Bottom line: she used what I call a kind of tough love to not punish but discipline her child. She wanted to quickly get her attention and immediately send home the message that if you play with fire, worse than this can happen to you. After she had given Lauren time to cry and process what had happened, she sat down with her and lovingly told her what she had done wrong and why she was spanked. Now, to me, this was one of the few times that spanking a child seemed appropriate.

Another example is my friend's story about his son, Jeremy. Jeremy was an active five year old who enjoyed playing games. He was in his front yard where a portable basketball goal was in the driveway. It was in a relatively safe place for Jeremy to play. The driveway was long and he had plenty of room to retrieve the ball. His father would often park the car in front of the driveway as a kind of shield to stop the ball if it ventured toward the street. More importantly, his father often played with him and his friends or was somewhere close to supervise the situation. On this particular day, he was planting some flowers in and around the porch area while a group of about six little boys played ball. It was a spirited game and at some point, one of the kids, in fun or frustration, kicked the ball toward the street. Jeremy went after the ball. The parked car serving as a shield was now a blind spot for the driver of a car coming up the road. He did not see the ball or Jeremy until it was almost too late. Although Jeremy had been told time and time again to stay out of the road and never to go into the street after the ball, he pursued the ball into the street. Only his dad's panic scream got the driver's and Jeremy's attention. It did not save the basketball, but the driver missed hitting Jeremy by a matter of inches. When his father witnessed all of this, he was scared, relieved, and frustrated at the same time. When he got to Jeremy, he sat down on the curb. With the yard gloves on his hand, he spanked Jeremy. Then, he literally cast him to the ground, looked at all the children who were playing, and reminded them how serious it is to run out into the street. He pointed out that a car accident could lead to a serious injury that could cause you to never to play with your friends again. He was quick to remind me that he never mentioned death and after he saw that his son was safe, he quickly regained his composure. He declared his spanking was hard and under control, but, for many reasons, that is the key. Again, it speaks to the child that what they have done must be something very serious. The parent, however, must remain under control because an out of control parent spanking a child can be serious.

First and foremost, you can physically hurt your child. While you want to get the child's attention and emotions and redirect his thinking, you do not want to physically hurt your child. Secondly, I reiterate that in most states it is against the law to physically hurt your child while spanking him or her.

Now, I have given you my examples of when I feel it is appropriate to actually put your hands on a child to discipline him. Let me give you another side of what I feel true disciplining is all about. Let me begin by saying that whereas you might punish a child too harshly, I do not believe you can over discipline a child. Naturally, you must let a child be a child (play, watch TV, and utilize technology). But, you are always in their lives, even if subtle, instilling good, strong, moral values. Proverbs uses the word "Train." Proverbs 22:6 declares, "Train up a child in the way he should go; and when he is old, he will not depart from it."

Perhaps punishment is a single act of hitting a child with a rod. Disciplining takes time and hard work. It could also become a great adventure. Let me give you my classic example of disciplining a child. A thirteen year old is caught smoking a cigarette in his backyard. Punishment would be a hitting with a rod or loss of privileges as no talking or texting on the phone or no TV privileges for a period of time. However, disciplining would be to voice your disappointment to the child. Then, take him to the library or to a cancer clinic where he gets information on the dangers of smoking. Take him to the store and get the price of his brand of cigarettes by the carton and have him add up the cost of his smoking on a monthly and yearly basis. Of course, all of this is awesome discipline if you are not a smoker yourself. Otherwise, you must join in this process with a commitment to your teen that you are giving up this deadly habit. After the child has done the research, perhaps you can take him to a clinic where he can see a lung that has been filled with smoke for years (which is grayish-black). Then, he can see a lung clear of smoke (which is clean and a light pink in color). Now, he can truly see for himself how cancer and emphysema come to be. This child could be required to do a written report on all the information he has gathered and what he has experienced. Remember, you have carried him through this process. Let his family be his audience as he talks from his written report about the dangers of smoking. Afterwards, perhaps you can talk with his teacher and he can make this same presentation to his health class at school. The whole process will probably take a couple of weeks, but can you imagine the impact it will have on him as he learns more and more about the dangers of smoking?

What's my point? Disciplining a child takes time. Disciplining is teaching and training so that a real learning process can take place. It is more than just a harsh word or a slap on the hand or bottom; rather, it is teaching a lesson that will hopefully stay with that child for a lifetime. Disciplining your child can and should be an awesome and powerful learning experience for all involved. However, it must be planned and void of anger, malice, or revenge. It might sound strange, but many a parent has entered into disciplining a child and ended up punishing a child beyond what was necessary because of anger. Therefore, I want to offer you these ten ways to control anger toward your children:

- Learn relaxation exercises and do them regularly to reduce anger before it builds up.
- Take time to cool off before you discipline your children.
- Do your best not to take your children's misbehavior personally.
- Keep in mind that we all slip up occasionally, including our children.
- Know what behaviors you must take a firm stand on and what you can be more flexible about.
- Look at the "big picture." If things are going well, do not make minor misbehavior big issues.
- Focus on your child's positive qualities and constructive behaviors.
- Remember that you serve as a model for your children. Think of how you would want them to handle their own anger.
- If you feel you need help in dealing with your anger or in disciplining your children, consider parenting classes or professional counseling.
- Make sure you get enough time away from your children to do things you enjoy so that parenting does not seem like a huge burden.

I believe discipline is the key to how we rear our children. I think it speaks volumes that a disciplined person will become a disciple of whatever the child is disciplined about. Think about it. Great athletes like Tiger Woods and Serena and Venus Williams were introduced to their particular sport when they were children. They grew up being disciplined about their sport. How awesome would children be if they could be taught to be disciplined in academics, social skills, the Christian faith, and money management, to name a few! Punishment must be the exception and not the rule. Be a disciplinarian and watch what God allows you to produce in a due season.

Chapter 4

<u>What You Need To Know About Gangs and Raising Children in a Postmodern World</u>

In the state of Georgia, we are very fortunate to have Officer Jesse Hambree of the Douglas County Sheriff's Office, Douglasville, Georgia. An expert in the field of gangs and violent behavior, he did his presentation at our church and at some of the Northwest Georgia Area schools on the Teachers' Training Days. He gave us a wealth of information on gangs and gang activity. It is that information that I now share with you.

WHAT IS A GANG?

Too many people believe the definition of a gang is a group of people who cause trouble or commit crimes or acts of violence. However, Georgia law is very specific about what a gang is. Georgia law states that a gang is: Three or more persons associated together by common name, hand signs, logos, tattoos, common colors, common clothing, or any other common characteristics engaging in crimes that are gang related. On a general and larger scale, we know this about gangs: According to the National Youth Gang Center, in 2006, there were approximately *785,000* active street gang members in the United States.

Los Angeles County is considered the *Gang Capital of America* with an estimated 120,000 (41,000 in the City) gang members although Chicago actually has a higher rate of gang membership per capita than Los Angeles. In addition, the state of Illinois has a higher rate of gang membership (8-11 gang members per 1,000 population) than California *(5-7* gang members per 1,000 population). There were at least 30,000 gangs and 800,000 gang members active across the USA in 2007. About 900,000 gang members lived "within local communities across the country," and about 147,000 in U.S. prisons or jails in 2009.

By 1999, Hispanics accounted for 47% of all gang members, Blacks 31%, Whites 13%, and Asians 6%.

STREET GANG IDENTIFICATION

Common Names: Most gangs choose a name for themselves: Bloods, Crips, Skin Heads, etc. to show allegiance to a specific geographical area or to relay a common belief system. Some choose to call themselves a music group, clique, or squad to avoid the stigma and attention of being called a gang. Most gang names are abbreviated into three or four letter combinations. Some of those abbreviations can be the same as other well known organizations to disguise the gang name and confuse others.

Hand Signs: Most gangs use hand signs as a common form of communication. Often, gang hand signs form numbers or letters to identify the group's name. Hand signs of one gang are very offensive to another and may incite tension and fights between the groups.

Symbols: Gangs can use any symbol to identify themselves. Sometimes, innocent looking symbols are used. Gangs may buy or design symbols for themselves. Some symbols are chosen based on their hidden meaning while others are quite obvious. Some symbols that look gang related may not be because of their other uses in the community.

Clothing: It is often very difficult to distinguish gang related clothing from current styles. Watch for members to wear the same colors all the time or at specific times, such as planned fights or when trouble occurs. Familiarize yourself with current gang clothing trends from internet sites or local law enforcement.

Colors: Gangs often decide on a common color that shows allegiance to a larger nationally known gang. While some gangs may choose two or three colors, colors mean very little to others.

Tattoos: Gang members will often tattoo, burn, or cut their gang name or logo onto their bodies. In some instances, non permanent ink markers are used instead of permanent markings.

Graffiti: Gangs will mark their area of operation with graffiti to let other rival gangs know who controls that area as well as to intimidate local citizens.

Social Websites: More commonly, gang members are using sites like MySpace and Facebook as places to show gang allegiance and group structure. Gang members often have pictures showing weapons, excessive money, and drug use to display gang names and other gang related behavior.

Now having shared this information, do not ever think gangs are not in your neighborhood. Moreover, please do not think that your child could not be a part of a gang group. Here are some warning signs to look for in an individual. Look for Graffiti (drawing names and symbols). Look for gang names, logos, and nicknames written on personal property. Observe withdrawal from family, friend, and normal activities being replaced by new friends that you, as a parent, do not know. When your child starts staying out later than the stated curfew and engages in secret activities, that is a red flag that something is going on. You might see sudden changes in behavior and personality with unexplained injuries, body markings, and tattoos. Children who are getting involved in gangs often receive unexplained gifts of money, expensive items such as jewelry, and/or possession of a weapon. Another obvious sign of gang involvement is the use of hand signs and/or body gestures when communicating with friends. Then, there is the preference for one color or avoidance of others. Finally, you know something is wrong when a child begins to skip school or work. More than likely, when there are multiple suspensions or expulsion, a show of strong disrespect for authority, use of drugs or alcohol, or mention of the need for a weapon or protection, you have a child who is involved with a gang.

Why do young people join gangs? Well, it is not necessarily any one person's fault, and perhaps there is enough blame to go around for everyone. The bottom line is young people have a lack in their lives and in some instances, they will do anything to fill that void. Some students have status, identity, or recognition issues. It could be a breakdown in the family. Some students suffer from low self-esteem, poor communication at home, and lack of success in school. Young people's need for acceptance and belonging are sometimes overwhelming.

Young people face peer pressure from gang groups and financial benefits from drug sales, burglaries, robberies, and other crimes.

Young people join a gang for protection and because other family members are already involved. Being in a gang gives some youngsters a sense of confidence, loyalty, rules, structure, discipline, and organization. Gang groups are attractive because they give a powerful group identity, relieve boredom, and create an opportunity to gain a reputation. These qualities are very appealing and attractive to young people; thus, they become involved in gang activities.

Now, the obvious question is, "What can parents do?"

- Develop open and frequent communications with your children.
- Encourage your children to become involved in other activities for a sense of belonging.
- Monitor and limit children's exposure to violence on television, in music, and video games.
- Cultivate respect for property and pride in the community.
- Know the real names of those your child is spending time with (and their families).
- Do not let children stay out late or spend a lot of time unsupervised.
- Become involved with your child's education and in your community.
- Praise your child for doing well.
- Spend quality time with your children and talk to them about gangs.
- Ask them their opinion about family matters.
- Identity with positive role models and be a good observer.
- Seek the facts: kids will tell you what you want to hear, and adults will believe what they want to hear.
- Set clear limits and follow through with proper discipline.
- Teach your children about decision making.
- Team up with other parents.
- Learn about gangs and drugs.

- Help develop alternatives for children in your neighborhood.
- Finally, monitor your child's internet activities and know what they are posting on the internet.

You are the parent and you are in charge. Be informed and make sure you develop and keep a strong relationship with your children.

Chapter 5

Mentoring and It's Impact Upon Our Children

What do we do when the family is absent of one or both of the parents? In the late 1950's and early 60's, it was hard for my mother to rear my brother and me. However, it worked because we had loving and caring grandparents to give her the support she needed. The African Proverb, "It takes a village to raise a child," was also in place. As pre-teens, we had about a mile long walk from our home to elementary school. It is a fact that the families knew each other and some were closer than others, but we were like a village. One thing is for sure. All of the parents knew the children well enough to discipline them to the point of a slap on the arm or leg if they were caught being mischievous. If a telephone call was made to your home, and this incident was reported, you were likely to get a real whipping or punishment for the bad behavior. Although most families did not have a lot of money, they had values and morals. You did not do wrong and get away with it. Discipline of some sort was the order of the day.

Also, in those days, we had good and bad role models. But, most were good. The preacher, barber, school teachers, business owners, doctors, grandparents, uncles, aunts and the like were close enough in the neighborhood that we could see them and say, "I want to be one of them when I grow up." Then, you could say that when one or both parents were absent, we had a great backup and support system. We had surrogate parents throughout the community.

Today, unfortunately, we do not have the same spirit about sharing and caring for children in the neighborhood. For one thing, we are not as neighborly. People are more private and intentionally distant from their neighbors, and that is with few exceptions. Families may be closer to families across town because they share some commonality; yet, they have little or no interaction with the neighbors next door. Today, an adult outside of a family would not think about disciplining another person's child. Throughout my entire public school life (k- 12thgrade), corporate punishment or paddling was a part of discipline. Today, however, very few school systems have the right to discipline a child by paddling. It is unacceptable. Whereas, I agree that paddling or spanking is not the answer (except in severe cases where the parents should do the spanking), there must be something in place that disciplines and gets a child's attention. If an "ounce of prevention is worth a pound of cure," consider this approach in helping children when there is either an absent parent or a child seems to have gone astray. Perhaps he or she can be helped with a mentor.

According to the American Heritage Dictionary, a mentor is a wise and trusted counselor or teacher. The word "mentor" has a Greek root meaning: steadfast and enduring. The Ancient Greek poet, Homer, first coined the word mentor in his epic poem, "The Odyssey". The great warrior, Odysseus, knew he would be away from home many years so he chose a man named Mentor to be the guardian and tutor for his son. Mentoring is a one-to-one relationship over a prolonged period of time between a youth and an older person, who provides consistent support, guidance and concrete help as the younger person goes through a difficult or challenging situation or period in life.

The goal of mentoring is to help the mentee (one being mentored) gain the skills and confidence to be responsible for his or her own future including an increased emphasis on academic and occupational skills. Mentoring is an act of community building. It requires believing in and caring about young people, their futures, and ours. Mentoring is the process of sharing personal knowledge and skills with a young person. Thus, mentor has come to mean any trusted counselor or guide. A mentor encourages his/her mentee to think, act, and evaluate. A mentor praises, prods, connects, and listens. A mentor helps a young person identify and develop his potential and shapes his life. A mentor encourages the mentee to use his strengths, to follow his dreams, and to accept his challenges.

"The true mentor fosters the young person development by believing in him, sharing his dream and giving it his blessing and helping to define the newly emerging self in its newly discovered world."

Daniel J. Levinson, The Seasons of a Man Life,

New York: Balantine, 1978.

WHY MENTORING?

Now, an obvious question is why mentoring? For one thing and like never before, there is an absence of authority figures in the lives of many children and teenagers. In the best of homes, some children have to go home from school to a house void of any guardian because the parents are at work and the relatives are across town. Children come from a house that is not always a home where there is love and concern. A growing population of children must call orphanages, foster homes, and places like Open Door Children's Home their permanent place of residence. These are not bad places, but they are not model homes. Other homes lack the presence of either parent, and many times, grandparents or another relative is left to rear a child. They love the child but lack the energy and know how in handling the postmodern day child and teenager.

Young people need and want support. The majority of young people cite parents or other adults as the first source of advice for troubling personal problems. Remember, there was a time when our society was made up of extended families and close communities. They not only had parents, but grandparents, aunts, uncles, older cousins and family friends who often naturally served as mentors.

In the late 1900's, the reality was this: Nationally, nearly 15 million children lived in single parent homes. Almost *2.5* million children under the age of 13 are unsupervised during a part of the day. Only 50 percent of all custodial mothers receive full payment of court-ordered support with *25* percent receiving nothing at all. One in five children lives in poverty. Only 40 percent of young people born in the U.S. can expect to spend their entire childhood living with both biological parents. Unfortunately, these figures are still rising.

THE ROLE AND REQUIREMENTS OF A MENTOR

Now, that is a general statement and before I go into detail, let me be clear as to what you must not do. You cannot and please do not give the impression that you can be all things to your mentee. I am telling you from experience. As a matter of fact, I was a lousy mentor. But, before long, I got better at it. Ultimately, I gave up being a mentor because I came to realize that it simply was not for me. My wife could have saved me a lot of heartache by reminding me that I was not always there for my own children like I should have been. I was a great provider, good disciplinarian, and motivator; but, I must confess that sometimes I was so busy being a Pastor that I missed a lot of precious time with my children. I missed some ball games, school presentations, and fun times around my home because I was busy being a Pastor. After about a decade in ministry, I finally learned that my first obligation as a minister was to be there for my family. I was not the focused parent I should have been and could have been. Later on in life when my children were out of the house and in college or grown, I became apart of the local 100 Black Men Organization. Nationwide, this group's first and foremost objective is to mentor students. Their motto is, "What they see they will be." It was through this organization that I learned what it meant to be a mentor. I attended the Rome-Floyd Mentor Program and was certified as a mentor. This meant taking classes and learning certain things that I will share momentarily. It also meant having a background check. Be very sure that anyone affiliated with your church, school, after school program, or any child friendly program has an official background check. Know who you are turning your children over to and remember that there are all kinds of predators waiting to prey on innocent children.

So there I was. I had my training, background check, my own children off to college, and a mindset to make a difference in a young boy's life. From hindsight, I now realize what I did not have was a patient heart to do mentoring appropriately and the ample time to be a good mentor. Remember, it takes one's willingness to give time to being a mentor because a mentor must ensure certain things are taking place in the mentee's life.

First and foremost, a mentor must see to it that his or her mentee has the academic support that's needed. You want to keep the student in school, helping them to graduate from high school. Sometime that means one on one help with that specific subject in which the mentee is weak. It means if you cannot help them, you will find them the help and be present with them. Then, you want to help them to evaluate educational choices. In other words, help them to answer the question, "Where do I go from here?" That means directing them to the available resources and preparing them for college exams, the military, or job options. Keep in mind that you want to make sure they have the options, not make the decisions for them.

Second in mentoring is being a role model. Role modeling is setting a proper example for your mentee. It is pointing out, demonstrating and explaining actions and values that enhance their chances for success and happiness. You want to help them to see and strive for broader horizons than what they presently see in their environment. Now, my problem as a role model was I could not encourage them without injecting my passion for my calling, which is that of a Pastor. You must be careful that you do not prompt your mentee to want to emulate you or your vocation. I was not aware that I was doing that until one of my mentees declared God had called him to preach. When that happened ,I knew in my heart that he did not fully grasp what he was saying or about to do. Five years down the road, he was no longer a preacher. He was also a broken young man. A mentor as a role model must model a good example, good behavior, positive thinking, and keep his mentee constantly exploring and asking the question, "Who am I and what do I really want to do with my life?" I think my problem was I did not know how to separate my mentoring from my ministry. I shared some things about my life and job that perhaps I should not have shared. I did not consciously want this young man to be a Pastor or Preacher, but I certainly emphasized to him that "there was no higher calling." Unconsciously, I must have persuaded him that he could not go wrong being a minister. When I tried to explain to him that it was indeed a calling from God, he was sure he had "heard the voice." Unfortunately, it was my voice he heard or he would still be preaching today. As a mentor, be a role model but be careful not to give too much information about your particular vocation. In other words, be careful not to get too close to your mentee. Concentrate on morals, values, dependability, and preparation, and be careful not to use your vocation as the prime or only example. That was my mistake. How can a mentor avoid the mistakes that I made? Learn to listen more than you talk. Use a proportionate amount of time listening to young people talk about their fears, dreams, and concerns. Sometimes, they get plenty of instructions, advice and direction, but you must also give them plenty of time to talk, vent, ask questions, and share their inner most feelings and concerns. You want to give the proper attention and concern.

Finally, know that it takes time to be a mentor. That is probably why I was not a good mentor, initially. I was often late for appointments or did not show up at all. I would call and give my apology, but that was not what they needed or deserved. Then, when I did show up after having missed earlier appointments, I would over compensate. I would make more promises than I could keep or buy them a gift that they did not necessarily need or deserve, but it made me feel better. A good mentor must be accountable. If you make a commitment for a meeting, activity, or any kind of appointment, make sure you keep your word. There is no excuse, barring an emergency. This consistent accountability has several benefits and it cements trust between mentor and mentee. Set a good example (role modeling) for young people to follow and set expectations that can be met. Remember, a mentor may be the only adult who really listens to him.

The United Way of America and the Enterprise Foundations sets forth "A Mentoring Program Manual" outlining "Qualities of Successful Mentors." These are listed below:

1. Personal commitment to be involved with another person for an extended time period - six month to one year minimum.
   Mentors have a genuine desire to be part of other people's lives, to help them win tough decisions, and to see them become the best they can be. They have to be invested in the mentoring relationship over the long haul. They have to be there long enough to make a difference.
2. Respect for individuals and for their abilities and their right to make their own choices in life.
   Mentors can't come with the attitude that their own ways are better or that participants need to be "rescued." Mentors who convey a sense of respect and equal dignity in the relationship win the trust of their partners and the privilege of being advisors to them.

3. Ability to listen and to accept different points of view

Most people can find someone who will give advice or express opinions. It's much harder to find someone who will suspend his or her own judgment and really listen. Mentors often help by simply listening, asking thoughtful questions, and giving participants an opportunity to explore their own thoughts with a minimum of interference. When people feel accepted, they are more likely to ask for and respond to good ideas.

4. Ability to empathize with another person's struggles

    Good mentors can feel with people without feeling pity "for" them. Even without having had the same life experiences, they can empathize with their partner's feelings and personal problems.

5. Ability to see solutions and opportunities as well as barriers

    Good mentors balance a realistic respect for the real and serious problems faced by their partners with optimism about finding equally realistic solutions. They are able to make sense of what seems to be a jumble of issues and point out sensible alternatives.

6. Flexibility and Openness

    Good mentors recognize that relationships take time to develop and that communication is a two-way street. They are willing to take time to get to know their partners, learn new things that are important to their partners (music, styles, and philosophies), and even be changed by their relationship.

Additionally, the Foundation defines the many roles of a mentor.

ROLES OF A MENTOR

- A Guide for the Mentee
- A Friend and Wise and Trusted Teacher
- A Cheerleader and Coach
- A Good Listener, Visionary, "Seer"
- A Confidant and Link to other Cultures
- A Role Model
- A Self-Esteem Booster and Tutor
- A Sounding Board, Brother and Sister

Though a mentor may be a role model, a true mentor does not ask another person to "be like me." A mentor says, "I will help you be whoever you wish to be."

Finally, a true mentor is a mentee. That is to say that I personally have at least two people in my life that I look to for advice, guidance, and direction. Then, I have several young men in ministry that I give advice, guidance, and direction about life and ministry. I hope I never get so old or wise that I will not look to someone older to advise me, and it remains my prayer that I might, in someway, mentor someone in my path.

Chapter 6

<u>Teen Abstinence...Goals to Set for Our Children</u>

Abstinence is the voluntary forbearance especially from indulgence of an appetite or craving or from eating some foods; the habitual abstaining from intoxicating beverages or sexual involvement. One of the good things about the Postmodern World is its Science and Technology. From this, we have also learned some very valuable information as to those things that can be detrimental to the welfare of our children and teenagers. Not only do we know what the problems are, but we have the solutions for them. Thus, the word abstinence becomes the key in bringing about changes in a hurting child's life and I will focus on two very important aspects: cravings for both food and sex.

On "Good Morning America" on February 9, 2010, Mrs. Michelle Obama announced what she called a "very ambitious" program to end the American plague of childhood obesity in a single generation. The far-reaching, nationwide campaign called "Let's Move" calls for a myriad initiative that targets what Mrs. Obama calls four key pillars: (1)getting parents more informed about nutrition and exercise, (2)improving the quality of food in schools, (3) making healthy foods more affordable and accessible for families, and (4) focusing more on physical education. "We all know the numbers," she said. "I mean, one in three kids is overweight or obese, and we're spending $150 billion a year treating obesity related illnesses. So we know this is a problem, and there's a lot at stake." I applaud and congratulate Mrs. Obama on her efforts to get children moving again and eating more nutritionally.

Obesity continued to increase dramatically during the late 1990's for Americans of all ages, according to the data collected and analyzed by the National Center for Health Statistics, part of the Centers for Disease Control and Prevention (CDC). The percent of children and teens that are overweight also continues to increase. Among children and teens, ages 6 - 19, 15 percent (almost 9 million) are overweight according to the 1999-2000 data, or triple what the proportion was in 1980. In addition, the data shows that another 15 percent of children and teens ages 6 to 19 are considered at risk of becoming overweight.

Obesity can be defined as an excessive accumulation of body fat which results in individuals being at least 20 percent heavier than their ideal body weight. "Overweight "is defined as any weight in excess of the ideal range. Obesity is a common eating disorder associated with adolescence. Although children have fewer weight-related health problems than adults, overweight children are at high risk of becoming overweight adolescents and adults.

Overweight people of all ages are at risk for a number of health problems including heart disease, diabetes, high blood pressure, stroke and some forms of cancer. Obesity can weaken physical health and well-being and shorten life expectancy. It can also lead to social disabilities and unhappiness which may cause stress and mental illness. A study released in May 2004 suggests that overweight children are more likely to be involved in bullying than normal-weight children are, both as victims and as perpetrators of teasing, name-calling, and physical bullying.

The development of a personal identity and body image is an important goal for adolescents. Parents, physicians, and teachers should work together to help youth to take off the weight and get up their self esteem.

Next is the age old discussion of teens being sexually active and the need for abstinence. Sexual abstinence among teens is more difficult now than perhaps anytime in world history. First and foremost, we must keep in mind that it is the teen age that is generally the beginning of the puberty stage. Merriam-Webster's dictionary defines puberty as "the condition of being or the period of becoming first capable of reproducing; sexually marked by maturing of the genital organs, development of secondary sex characteristics, and in the human and in higher primates by the first occurrence of menstruation in the female; The age at which puberty occurs often construed legally as 14 in boys and 12 in girls." We know that puberty actually occurs much younger in some children. The point I make is this: at the puberty stage, children/teenagers naturally become curious about their bodies and the bodies of the opposite sex. Today, in the postmodern world, there is a real curiosity for experimenting with the opposite sex, but, some same sex relationships occur doing this early stage as well. I've been told by some teens that some same sex activity, especially among girls, occurs because there is gratification with no fear of pregnancy.

This is the nature of sexuality. That is to say, it comes naturally. Therefore, there is a need to inject spirituality into our sexual behavior. Rev. Annie Carter, the former Coordinator of Health Ministry at Saint Luke AME Church, Cartersville, Georgia, gives tremendous insight into this train of thought. Rev. Annie Carter once spoke at our World Aids Day and said, "Love is not sexual; love is spiritual." Wrapped around this statement was the idea that children start off in the wrong direction about sex because they get little or no instructions from parents as to what their sexuality is really all about. I must admit when I went through puberty, neither my father nor mother was in my life. I lived with my grandparents. My grandfather said absolutely nothing to me about how to interact or to refrain from getting too involved with girls. One day my grandmother told me (and it seems as an after thought), "Boy, don't get none of these girls pregnant. If you do, you'll be getting a job and moving out of here." That was my education from my parents on sex, and my parents and grandparents genuinely loved me. But, that was all they knew to tell me. So, this was Rev. Carter's train of thought, "Children/teens do not get the needed encouragement, education, and training about what is going on with their bodies at puberty, and how to deal with the attraction to the opposite sex or same sex. Where do they get it? They get their information, for the most part, from their peers, television, music, and the world around them." So many children grow into puberty literally left alone to figure out what is happening to them. True sexuality is private, personal, and intimate and should be treated as such. When those elements are talked about and reinforced throughout the puberty period by parents, other informed adults, and maybe older siblings, sex can then be viewed as a sacred, spiritual encounter to be regarded as special. It becomes something for which you wait for a special person to enjoy. It is, indeed, about love and spirituality, and becomes the gift that God intended it to be. However, we have a long way to go to get that word out to our children. Too many parents say nothing about it. The school classroom is often too clinical and many pastors rarely talk about sex from the pulpit.

So, for moral and health reasons, as well as a standard of life, we must teach our teenagers to embrace sexual abstinence. The obvious question is how? How do we give our children a real chance to understand sex and their sexuality in times like these when such activities are no longer confined to the bedroom between a married man and woman? Without hesitation, I can say that parents and guardians are the first place at which to start this process. Parents, it is ok for you to talk to your children about sex. It might seem awkward at first, but help each other to get past the embarrassing, uncomfortable, and uneasy feeling both parents and children might have. Talk to them about it regularly and at the appropriate times. Children want to talk about it. You can do it as a group discussion, and some times you can break the group up along gender lines for more private and intimate conversations if you feel that it is needed. However, you must be open and real with your children about this subject. Now, I am not saying that the conversation should be 'off the cuff' anything goes kind of conversation. Nor am I saying that it should be like a devotional period. Just be real, honest, and sincere. Come up with a plan that will allow you to share together the truth about puberty and how the body changes. Who knows your children better than you? Therefore, you will sense how much information to give them on particular subjects at the appropriate time. Pray about this because timing is important. Ensure there's not too much information, not too little information, but just enough at the right time. You know your child better than anyone so you can sense when it is time to move to the next issue and to another level of information. Parents, it is ok to be transparent. Share some of your experiences at the appropriate time. There are books available that give details about the male and female body and sex organs. Read through those kinds of books with them. Then, have discussion about what you have read. There are videos out there that can help in the education process. Watch them together. Also, watch fictional movies that tell the story of the heartache and pain inappropriate sexual acting out can do to a family. Perhaps, you may know of a true story that you can share that again reinforces abstinence. Let them see examples of how it disrupts the family and how everyone who loves the individuals involved is hurt behind unwanted pregnancies, sexually transmitted diseases, guilt, and shame. There are some good movies out there that make those points. Some movies, unfortunately, glamorize fornication, homosexuality, adultery, etc.; so, make sure you have reviewed your movies before you share.

The process of sharing information and being open to listening to youth issues about the subject of sexual abstinence should be ongoing until they are mature and strong in decision making for themselves. Eventually, it comes down to simply helping our youth to make good decisions when you are not around and they are on their own. You want your influence from home to be greater than the influence of peers and the other voices outside the home. Now, if you want some specific topics to talk about with those young teens, start by raising this question: Why do young people become sexually involved? When you help them to answer that question and questions like that, then, you can give them the social, psychological, or health gains to be realized by abstaining from sexual activity.

It is also most important to dispel myths about sex and identifying alternative ways of meeting personal needs. Examples of such myths are: I cannot get pregnant my first time; I cannot get pregnant if I have sex standing up; I cannot get pregnant if I have sex in water, or having sex makes a teenager an adult.

Call it innocent, puppy love, girlfriend/boyfriend love, or BFF, teens are going to want to be together and get to know each other so you must help provide alternative ways of meeting those personal needs. Know your children's friends. Help them with planning and doing things together. Get them involved in positive activities. Perhaps, they can learn to cook for each other, help each other with school work, go to church together, or get involved with other agencies that promote the idea of being friendly but practice and promote abstinence. Now, keep in mind, you are overseeing all of this. You will learn to trust your children and their friends, and they will learn to trust you and confide in you as they mature and begin to reach some of their goals.

You can also tell your teenager what God has said about the institution of marriage (2nd Chapter of Genesis and Matthew the 19th chapter). Share with them the story of Sodom and Gomorrah and your interpretation of it and what it means in these days and time. You do not have to agree on everything, but you must get the information out to them. Remember, the whole point of this is to help them guard their future and for them to have a good life. Again, on a personal note, let me reinforce to you that as a parent, you must keep your children busy doing positive things. I was an awesome parent when it came to making money to provide for them. However, I must admit that often times, I would lose my way when it came to spending quantity and quality time with my children. Thank God for my wife who filled the void and went beyond the call of duty. Many times, she was indeed mama and daddy. That's not to say I was a bad parent. I simply did not understand that my first calling as a minister was to be an example of a believer to my family first. One thing my wife did was to keep our children busy. They were expected to do well in school; therefore, homework was a must. Then, the day was extended with all kinds of afterschool activities such as sports, library, youth activities at church, music lessons, and putting on their own talent shows. Our children were kept busy. If you are too busy to spend quality and quantity times with your children, you are indeed too busy.

One final thought for every parent: Know where your children are at all times. Yes, from the cradle to the first day of college, know where your children are. This is not hard if you plan it. If you plan it from the cradle, they will come to accept it. Let them know it is not a matter of distrust; rather, it is a matter of love. It is taking care of your investment. If you are spending time with them, molding them, and shaping their lives, you are indeed their mentors. They will not mind that at all. The question often raised is: "Can you be your child's parent and friend at the same time?" I suggest that you can if you are the parent first. That is to say as long as they understand you are the leader of the pack, and you must do what is parental over what seems friendlier. However, the love is always there. It takes teamwork between the parents to know where your children/teenagers are at all times. So, you bought your son a car. How can you know where he is? Well, he's always going to tell you where he's going, and from time to time, you are going to literally check on him. If he misses being at the appointed place, you do what the good Lord does from time to time. Remember, our Lord's example about life: "The Lord giveth and the Lord taketh away." Then, you talk to your son or daughter in a language that he or she understands because you are having these talks anyway. He does not want to let you down. All teens do at some time challenge authority, see how much they can get away with; or another way to say it is "sow their wild oats." Yet, most teenagers generally love and respect their parents. You have taught them to respect and honor you. Parents, it is the calling of your life to rear your children in the way they should go. Parents, it is your duty to bring them up in the admonition of the Lord. They will grow to be what they see. They will grow to be whatever you help them to be.

Finally, keep the lines of communications open. Dare to talk to your children about anything and everything. Some subjects will be difficult, but you can get through it because it is not just an every now and then discourse. It is daily conversations of giving and receiving information from one another. It is growing together as you train your children to live a life that is pleasing in the eyes of God and most rewarding and beneficial for them. Your children not only need your direction, they want your direction and influence in their lives. They may not ever admit it while under your roof, but ultimately, they really want to be like you. A friend of mine shared these words with me recently: "Spend quantity time with your children, and the quality time will manifest itself". Remember to keep them covered in prayer. Then they will learn to abstain from those things that can harm and destroy them. These principles apply not only to what they eat and sexual abstinence, but smoking, drug use and other bad habits as well. In other chapters, I will give more detail on how you can create an atmosphere for children/teens to abstain from other negative influences.

Chapter 7

The Greatest Problem Children Face In The Postmodern World

For more than a decade, I have been blessed to be a part of a summer camp at our church. Beginning on the first Monday in May after school is out until the Friday in July before school begins, our summer camp provides a safe haven for school age children (ages six to eighteen). Over the years, I have come to realize that some students overwhelmingly act inferior to others while others dominate with words or antics. In the process, I noticed that so many of our children have limited social skills, communication skills, as well as no real understanding about what life is all about. So as I observed this, I saw the need to develop a class that I call "Creative Thinking".

My "Creative Thinking" class has two main objectives: (1) encouraging students to write a response to open ended, critical thinking questions. The questions asked require them to think about life and plans for their future. (2) Teaching and stressing the importance of communication skills by allowing students to make oral presentations to the class. My purpose for this class is to provide some resolve to what I am suggesting is the greatest problem a child/teenager faces in the Postmodern World and that is the problem of self-esteem.

SELF – ESTEEM

From Wikipedia Encyclopedia, Self-esteem is a term in psychology to reflect a person's overall evaluation or appraisal of his or her own worth. Self-esteem encompasses beliefs (for example, "I am competent", "I am worthy") and emotions such as triumph, despair, pride and shame. The self-concept is what we think about the self; self-esteem, the positive or negative evaluation of the self, is how we feel about it. So the ultimate goal for the "Creative Thinking" class is to encourage, inspire, and boost self-esteem in the students. I want to believe that we have had some success but I have not come up with a way to chart the students' progress. Hopefully, time will tell by their actions and reactions to things they do and by the way they handle specific situations.

HERE ARE SOME OF THE ITEMS I HAVE ASKED THEM TO ADDRESS:

1. What are some things that can get you into trouble (serious trouble)? How do you avoid trouble? What are your values (what is really important to you)? Where do you draw the line?
2. What is life and what does it mean to you? At the end of life what do you want people to remember about you? What is your greatest desire? Who, other than God, can help you fulfill your dreams?
3. Write a Story: If you could go anywhere in the world, where would you go? Who would you take with you? What would be your purpose?
4. Who are the three most important people to you and why?
5. If you had a million dollars what would you do with it and why?
6. What are your plans for the future and how will you make them happen?
7. Name three famous people who have affected your life in some way?
8. If you could be anybody in the world (dead or alive) who would it be and why?
9. In your opinion, name three of the greatest leaders. Now tell me what characteristic traits they have that make them great leaders.
10. In your opinion, what's wrong with the world? If you could change some things in the world, what would you do to make the world a better place?
11. I hope you live to be 99 years old, but if you died today what would your legacy be?
12. Give us an original statement of wisdom. If you were giving someone encouragement about how to live life, what would be your advice to your peers?
13. You are not homeless, but your family income is really low. It is so hard for them to make ends meet and you are thinking now it is

time for you to step up to the plate. What can you do (LEGALLY, WITHIN THE LAW) to bring some income into your household?
14. What can and what will you do to make (1) things better for your family, (2) things better for your friends, and (3) things better for you? In other words list at least three things you know you can do that will make you a better person and how will you begin to implement these things?
15. Write a poem that expresses your feelings about life, yourself, your family, and friends or perhaps some personal point of view on any subject. It must be at least 6 – 8 sentences. (see if you can make it rhyme)
16. Who is a leader? Are leaders born or made?
17. For you, is being a leader a natural gift or do you have to work at it?
18. You've had this job for 3 months and you enjoy it and need the money. However, your boss has told your team of 5 that he must release 2 of you. Persuade your boss that you are worth keeping.
19. You have had this friend for years, but now he or she is doing things that you want no part of doing. Experimenting with alcohol and drugs, and now getting involved with sexual activities is just not something you are ready for. Without seeming ugly, arrogant, or rude, how do you tell them that you do not want to be their friends, at least as long as they are doing things that are not right for you?
20. You want to get a Tattoo. Your parents told you long ago to never ask for a tattoo as long as you live with them. State your case to them as to why you feel justified in having a tattoo.

Finally, as an instructor, the most important thing I can do is to raise awareness about life, life concerns, and what's important to them. I present the questions, but let them formulate the answers. When necessary I redirect them, seek more information from them, and encourage them that their values, opinions and feelings count. I am confident that when a student thinks and writes down the answer to questions (relevant questions concerning their lives), then stand before his/her peers and gives a presentation on the subject matter, they grow and mature intellectually. In other words they develop self-esteem.

You want to stop **"Bullying"**? Help the students to develop self-esteem. I noticed that it works for the giver and the receiver of bullying. A bully who comes to have more self-esteem does not waste his/her time putting others down. A person that is bullied learns not to pay attention to someone bullying them if they are secure in who they are. It takes time, but it works. If we raise and build self-esteem in our youth; then character, integrity, fortitude, and positive thinking will follow. We can and must inspire our children that they can do all things through Christ who strengthens them. (Philippians 4:13) That's my definition of "Self-Esteem".

An inspirational movie for anyone (children especially) is "Akeelah and the Bee", directed by Doug Atchison. Keke Palmer plays the starring role, and Angela Bassett and Lawrence Fishburne are the co-stars. In the movie when Mr. Larabee triess to encourage Akeelah, he uses these words: "Our deepest fear is not that we are inadequate. Our deepest fear is that we are powerful beyond measure. It is our light, not our darkness, that most frightens us. We ask ourselves, who am I to be brilliant, gorgeous, talented, and fabulous? Actually, who are you not to be? You are a child of God. Your playing small does not serve the world. There is nothing enlightened about shrinking so that other people won't feel insecure around you. We are all meant to shine, as children do. We were born to make manifest the glory of God that is within us. It's not just in some of us; it's in everyone. And as we let our own light shine, we unconsciously give other people permission to do the same. As we are liberated from our own fear, our presence automatically liberates others." —from ***A Return to Love***, by Marianne Williamson. Mr. Larabee tells Akeelah that the meaning of that saying was: You don't have to be afraid of "Me" (me being yourself).

Remember this line from the movie, "The Help". "You is smart, you is kind, and is important". That may be broken English, but the message is good for character building. In the spirit of such movies as "Akeelah and the Bee" and "The Help", we must teach our children to think well of themselves at all times.

There was a Pastor that mentored me for years through the vehicle of raising questions. He never tried to control my life or tell me what I needed to do; he simply raised questions that caused me to think for myself and to draw my own conclusions. I believe that is one way we help our children and teenagers today by raising appropriate questions. I am suggesting that is a basis or growth process for helping our children to make good choices. Help them to think by constantly raising questions for their consideration.

Chapter 8

A Children's Ministry and It's Impact Upon One's Church and Community

One of the greatest decisions I have made during my 26 years as pastor of the Lovejoy Baptist Church was to ensure a solid children's ministry. When I came to the church, my children were 6, 8, and 10 years old. The congregation also consisted of children that age and older. It only made sense to enhance the programs we had such as Sunday School, Vacation Bible School, and a Children and Youth Choir. It was fun watching these organizations grow. My best help was the youth themselves. One of the things I did as I was led of the Holy Spirit to do was to make every fourth Sunday "Youth Sunday." This was the Sunday the children and youth were in charge of every facet of the worship service including the devotional service which led to our having what we called "Junior Deacons." A young person would be the presiding officer; another would read the scripture, and someone would be given the task of leading us in congregational prayer. Our youth choir would sing and our youth usher ministry served. The bottom line is that once a month, our young people could exercise their gifts and talents. This fourth Sunday tradition continues to this day. In this Postmodern World, the church must do all it can to reach young people for Christ. If I had known that we would have been so faithful and successful in our efforts to reach young people, I would have kept better records of our progress. Just know that most of the children who grew up in the church have also been blessed to go on to college and are doing well.

Now, I want to share some ideas as to how you can start youth ministries in your church. First and foremost, do not attempt to start anything at the church without the pastor's permission and blessings. If you get that, you are halfway there. You can never succeed without your pastor's support. He or she can reach people that you cannot reach. The pastor can help make the vision real and promote the idea every Sunday from the pulpit, and you cannot. Further, he or she is the spiritual leader, and any activity in the church must have leadership blessing.

If you want to jump start a program and get people excited about it, name your youth program or youth ministry in honor of someone beloved in the church. They could be deceased or still alive. The key to it is they should be one of those faithful members that everyone has come to love and respect over the years. There was such a pastor of Lovejoy named Reverend J.L. Vaughn,Sr. Reverend Vaughn pastored the church for over 50 years. When I was led of God to start a tape ministry, I called it the "Reverend J.L. Vaughn Tape Ministry". All proceeds from the tape ministry go to a scholarship fund to help students who attend Lovejoy to attend college or vocational school. This has lead to the Reverend J.L. Vaughn Tracking and Scholarship Ministry. All children attending our church are monitored by this program. If they need tutoring, we provide it. We help them prepare to take the SAT or ACT College Prep Exams. Financially, we fund the cost of the pre-college exams. All of this is done in the name of Reverend J.L. Vaughn because when he was a pastor, he certainly promoted education in the community. That is my classic example.

For more than three decades, his daughter-in-law played for our church, and now, she plays for us on a part-time basis. When she had officially retired, "The Esther S. Vaughn Fine Arts Program" was established in her honor. The truth is that before it was ever named, she began giving her pay from playing the organ of the church to helping our youth take piano lessons. This blossomed into a program that now offers piano lessons, drum lessons, singing lessons, dancing lessons, and other instrument lessons to deserving youth. This is all because a lady wanted to ensure that the music ministry of the church would be expanded and reach out to children. This program continues to flourish. We see the results around the church through our music department. Starting youth ministries in honor of faithful members is surely a way to get that ministry off the ground.

So, in the Postmodern World where there seems to be no particularly absolute truths among our youth, we must have ministries that call their attention to Biblical truths that instill morals and boost morale. Churches must have ministries that teach Jesus Christ and His principles that can be absorbed into their lives by the indwelling of the Holy Spirit. To say it another way, the church must lead our children to Christ that they might be saved.

Starting a Children's Ministry is an excellent way to attract young families to your church and to keep them coming back for more. Taking the time to properly begin the ministry will ensure a thriving ministry and excellent growth potential for the church. Here are the steps to organize your children's ministry:

1. Form a team. The team should be made up of several members of the congregation from a varied age range. Most importantly, they must be willing to share your vision, and you must know they will work with you. Include, for example, a mom of a pre-school student, a dad of a middle school student, and parents of elementary and high school students. Grandparents, educators, and Sunday school teachers from the congregation should also be included. Do not forget to invite the pastor. If he or she chooses not to be directly involved, keep the pastor informed of your progress.
2. Start with a vision statement. A vision statement is your written plan for the future. It must be plain, simple, and to the point. You may have a general statement like: "Lovejoy Baptist Church shall meet the spiritual needs of the children in and around our church community. We shall have a weekly agenda that will allow children access to vital church programs at least 5 days per week. Our goal is to save the Children to Christ, then nurture them to become mature disciples of Christ." "Train up a child in the way he should go, and when he is old he will not depart from it" (Proverbs 22:6).
3. Evaluate your present Children's Ministries. If some program is "not broken, don't fix it." Improve on programs where you can, but most of all, try to find new programs (one program at a time) that are different and more challenging than present programs. For example, if your church does not have any type of after school program, perhaps you might consider organizing a 4 day a week program for a couple of hours where a snack is served. Schedule 1/2 hour of academics, 1/2 hour of a scriptural/moral lesson, and

perhaps some recreational time. You do not have to keep the children for a long period of time. Provide an activity that is unique and special when they are in attendance. Finally, have a plan in place to allow for ongoing evaluation. You want to keep your programs interesting. The students will always look forward to getting back to church and to the program if these things are done.

4. Investigate other Children's Ministries. If you see a program at another church, online, on television, or if you should read about one, do not hesitate to emulate that program. You do not have to do it exactly like others do, but make it suit your needs. It's just like the sermons I hear. If it touches my spirit to preach it, I do. I just make sure that I make it mine. I study the scripture, then I use what suits me from the sermon I heard, adding what the Holy Spirit gives me. Do that with your Children's Ministries. You do not have to re-create the wheel.

5. Develop a plan. Now, it's time to move from the general to the particulars. You have looked at your children ministries, other children's ministries, and your vision statement. Now, it is time to make a list and enter into a step by step process of establishing a program. Remember, for best results, do one new program at a time. Once a program is in operation and stable, look at another project.

6. Budget. Find out how much money you are going to need to start your program. If you do not have those funds, it is time for a fundraiser. Remember, you might name the child's ministry after some beloved person in the church. Have a special day for them. Give them an honorarium, but let all the other proceeds go to your program. You might solicit monthly sponsors. Make sure your sponsors know this must be above and beyond what they give in tithes and offerings. A car wash, movie night, and other fundraisers can support your program and get the youth involved.

7. Seek out a teaching staff. The teachers are there in your congregation. Ask some of the retired teachers, present Sunday school teachers, as well as those who teach school now. The only

thing you look for in a teacher is that they have a heart for a children's ministry and like working with children. If they share your vision, they can teach or they can help to qualify teachers for your program.
8. Prepare a calendar. First and foremost, plan your program when it is convenient for the teachers and students. Sometimes, it is good to have limited days and times; then, let it grow. Avoid those times during vacation seasons and holidays.
9. Continue to Set Goals. As your programs take off, be more specific in purpose and refine your plan to meet age group needs as well as the individual needs of children. Goals need to be specific, measurable, biblical, and attainable. Every age group will not achieve every goal, but the ministry as a whole should be regularly meeting designated goals. Remember, we are called to be faithful; success is in God's hand.
10. Form a Publicity Committee. Find someone around the church who has marketing skills. You want to be able to publicize your ministries so that people will come to the church and be blessed. It must be presented in the church bulletin, local newspaper, radio, and on the internet. In fact, the internet will allow you to witness for Christ to those who might not be able to actually come to the programs. It might inspire someone in another church to improve their church youth ministries. Nothing impresses people like watching children happy at play around a church. Think about that.
11. PRAY. Keep your program, program leaders, teachers, students, pastor and congregation in your prayers. God's divine intervention is the ultimate key to a Godly children's ministry.

I am so blessed to be a part of and nurturer of the youth program around our church. I would like to think that we have and are doing an adequate job of what is called the "holistic approach" to nurturing children. That is, we have something to offer every age group at our church until they leave for college, the military, vocational school, or the workforce. It starts with our nursery for ages three months to three years. Then, they move to our children's church that is for ages four to seven. We have Wednesday night classes for pre-school, elementary, middle, and high school level students. Sometimes, we will separate the high school girls and boys in order to have more intimate conversation on personal subjects. We are also blessed to take a percentage of our students to the National Baptist Congress of Christian Education held annually in a different major city. Yes, we have fundraisers all through the year. The student must not only help in these efforts, but they must also be present for church functions at least 80% of the time. We have done this for more than a decade, and I know some of our youth have had life changing experiences. Some, perhaps, would not have had the opportunity to see a large metropolitan city or to be a part of a dynamic program that involves thousands of children and youth working together to accomplish the end of the week "Rally."

Lovejoy 's crowning jewel in this effort is one of our students who started going on these trips and received his call into the ministry at the age of **15**. Reverend Brandon Crowley became a standout student at Morehouse College, where he graduated with honors. He is now pastor of Myrtle Baptist Church in West Newton, Massachusetts, a graduate of Harvard University with a Master of Divinity degree as well as a graduate of Boston University with a Master of Sacred Theology degree. His goal is to acquire a PH.D degree and teach on the college level as he continues his pastoral career. We pray Reverend Crowley continues to build on the legacy of what can happen when a child is given a chance. Crowley came to Lovejoy Baptist Church about a year after I became pastor. He joined the church at approximately **5** years old and I have been blessed to watch him grow and mature in Christ.

My point is that the church has a responsibility and obligation to have ministries that will make a difference in the life of a child.

There is one final thought I want readers to consider. If you feel that organizing a children's ministry is more than your church can do alone at this point, there is another alternative of getting Christian influence to our children. It is called Partnering. You may not have total control or influence; however, you can be effective in touching the lives of children in a positive way. Let me give you an example of what I call partnering.

Partnering is a church or any other institution joining forces with other institutions or agencies to aid or supplement a school, recreation department, Boys and Girls Club, YMCA, or any other institutions for children or teen-agers. For example, our church is a Partner in Education with Anna K. Davie Elementary School, located right around the corner from our church. It is the neighborhood school in the South Rome Community. The students who attend this school come from moderate to low income families. Large percentages are single parent families. Another section is the Hispanic population and the parents who do not speak English. Yet, in spite of all these negative factors, this school was recently recognized in the local newspaper for being a "No Excuses School," signifying the academic success of the students in spite of the negative factors affecting the maturation of the students. This school has at least three partners: Lovejoy Baptist Church, 100 Black Men of Rome, Incorporated, and Georgia Power. On a quarterly basis, 100 Black Men of Rome Incorporated meet and coordinate what each will do to help the school. For example, it has been our job to sponsor food for PTA meetings. This almost ensures the presence of parents and students where valuable information is given out and important decisions are made. The church's Life Center is always available to the school for banquets and end of year programs. As a pastor, I am called upon for the school's annual "Career Day." We also make financial contributions for purchasing books, supporting field trips, and providing other needs.

The 100 Black Men of Rome, Incorporated is a mentoring group. They are in various schools on a weekly basis spending one on one time with students who have been identified as those most in need of this help. They have started a Reading Club and a Writers' Academy. Both of these programs enhance the participant's skills and increase their chances of success in these areas as they matriculate through the year. They often have "Weiner Roast Day" just for the fun of it. It gets the parents, teachers, and students out on the lawn to just have fun and fellowship.

Georgia Power is the other partner in education. While they are not as visible as other partners, they provide a lot of funding. Purchasing books, sponsoring trips, and doing special things for the staff is their specialty. They also bring their trucks out on career day and explain to the students just how Georgia Power serves the community and state. Partnering Works! It takes the load off one institution and allows for several institutions to seriously impact a school or other student oriented programs. We also partner with our neighborhood Boys and Girls Club and basically provide the same things for this organization. Every church should be challenged to get involved through partnering. A simple phone call to the school administrator can get the ball rolling. Find other agencies interested in the school and get them involved as well.

Chapter 9

Rearing Sheri, The Little Girl Who Lived At Our House

Nick and Lori had already reared their three children. Nick was a successful business man and a deacon in the church. She was a nurse in a children's hospital and a Sunday School teacher. Nick had a niece named Brenda who had fallen upon hard times. She was trying to rear three children by herself, two teenagers and an eleven year old. Brenda had minimal job skills and a support system that primarily consisted of her mother. One afternoon, in hopes of giving Brenda some relief, Lori had gone to visit them and asked if the youngest child, Sheri, could come over and spend the weekend with her and Nick.

Ever since, Sheri has been with Nick and Lori. This was not what Lori intended, and she had expressed that to Nick on several occasions. Lori understood very clearly the tremendous responsibility in rearing a child/teenager in these days and times. Besides, both Nick and Lori were in their late 40's, and they had reared their children. They had made the transition from a full house to an empty nest. Lori looked forward to grandchildren. Grandchildren are just that, she thought… GRAND. Furthermore, you can always take them home to their parents. Rearing a grand niece was not in her plans. On the other hand, Nick had just lost his mother. As a way of dealing with his grief, he immediately transferred his desire to share and care from his mother to his grand niece.

Whereas Nick welcomed the idea of someone else in the house to love, Lori felt she now had to compete for her husband's attention. Lori loved her great niece, but she also loved her freedom to come and go as she desired. She felt Nick's thinking was clouded by grief. He was too emotional to think rationally. However, it was Lori who brought her to their home and made the proposal that she stay for a while.

So, how did they end up keeping this child? As one weekend turned into weeks and months, they began to see a physically pretty little girl who was also a troubled little girl. Sheri had been tested at school and had no obvious mental or emotional problems. Tests showed Sheri's IQ to be slightly below normal for her age. She had failed the third grade only because of poor attendance. She was functioning below grade level, did not like school, and frequently acted out at school. At home, Nick and Lori noticed that Sheri had mood swings. Some days she would have a happy go lucky disposition, and other days, she was quiet and seemed somewhat depressed. She seemed indifferent to the fact that she was living in a home where she had her own room, bathroom, and her own den area with TV, telephone, and computer. During her first Christmas at their home, she received and X-Box, a bicycle, and clothes.

When Sheri entered the sixth grade, it was at a new school. She began learning to play the clarinet. She was in a home where they prayed together most every morning. She attended Sunday School and church every Sunday. Slowly but surely, Sheri's behavior improved. It was obvious, however, that something was still lacking in her life that was causing some bad behavior, sudden outbursts, and depression.

Sheri continued visiting her mom and siblings. Nick and Lori observed that often when Sheri returned from visits with her family, she would seem depressed as if she missed being with her biological family. However, her mom often stated that Sheri was almost always eager to return to her home with Nick and Lori. It was these visits that allowed Nick and Lori to come to understand what Sheri's basic problem was. She had not experienced real stability in her life. She was now a 13 year old who had lived in two cities and moved from one home to another, often moving back to her grandmother's home because of her mom's struggle to raise her family. Sheri had attended four schools in six years. The bottom line was that this girl (like so many little girls and boys in our society today) had lived a life where the only constant things in her life were uncertainty and instability. Her families love for her was unquestionable. So, could her inability to learn be linked to the fact that she had more important things on her mind? Things like "will my mom be alright, what are we going to eat, and where are we going to live" might have been heavy on her mind. Could her depression and acting out behavior simply be Sheri's way of coping and surviving in a world full of uncertainty and change? Sheri also had a way of always shifting the reasons for her actions to someone else. If she got into trouble at school, it was always another student's fault, or "the teacher just does not like me" would be her response. They even recognized this pattern at home.

Once Sheri got comfortable with her new guardians, she did what most or many children attempt to do at some point or another, and that is to pit one parent against the other. "Well, Nick said I could go to Sharon's house if I was good today." Lori's reply, "But you have not been good and you are not going anywhere." So, Sheri would run to Nick upset and crying, "Nobody loves me and nobody will give me a chance, especially Lori. Everybody is always picking on me." This is generally true when children enter the teen years or that time of puberty. Not only do their bodies begin to physically change (estrogen and testosterone kicking in), they also begin to think they are invincible. Oftentimes, this means they will not listen to reason because their minds are made up as to what they want to do or what they think is best for them. They think if anyone comes against them, someone else is wrong and others are to blame. It is about me and what I want to do. If anyone comes against them, they are wrong, and others are to blame for all their troubles. Nick and Lori began to see that in their thirteen year old niece. The good part is that they had seen it before. They had heard the story of, "I did not clean up the kitchen last night because I was doing my homework and fell off to sleep," or "I was going to wash the clothes, but I could not find the washing powder." Yet, the washing powder is found on the top shelf where it always is when not in use. "Well, the reason I missed the school bus home is because John had my jacket and would not give it back and I was running after him. The bus driver saw me, but he pulled right off and left me. I do not know why he would do me that way."

I am sure that most parents have experienced this kind of scenario (or something similar) in their relationship with their children. The idea is that what is wrong is always something or somebody else's fault. I call it playing the "Blame Game." It is from this situation that I offered Nick and Lori some help for Sheri with a program called the "Point and Level

System". I learned about this program while teaching behavior disorder students in a local high school. The program consisted of students who had been diagnosed as having some type of emotional problem. I came to realize that once you discover the students' individual needs and give them patience, structure and stability, they respond and are quite normal. They still have the same issues as all children/teenagers have. I concluded that programs like the Point and Level System will work for most teenagers. I say most because the teenager has to embrace it for it to work. I have watched this process literally change lives as well as make matters worst. It simply depends on the individuals working with it.

The Point and Level System is a program that literally holds the teenager responsible for his or her behavior. This program may work with some pre-teens. It works best with a child who is mature enough to see that the work is worth the reward.

It is the parents' responsibility to set up a list of chores at home, expectations for school, the neighborhood, church, and any other place they choose to monitor behavior or set expectations. They must then work with the teenager to come up with a reward system for acquiring a certain amount of points for completing the assigned tasks. A certain amount of points will determine a certain level, and the higher the level, the greater the reward. Each time the child accomplishes a particular goal, he receives points. The more points earned will place him on a higher reward level, and a lack of points will disqualify him from getting any rewards. These chores and expectations should be examined on a daily basis. After a period of time, (generally on a weekly basis) the parents and teenager should sit down and review the week's activities and determine the level the teen is on (according to the points earned) for the upcoming week, thereby, receiving the reward(s) given for being on that level. However, greater than the level or reward is the fact that the program literally teaches a child to be responsible and accountable. If he or she gets to a certain level, he or she is rewarded. If not, he or she has no one to blame but himself. Below is an example of the Point and Level System. It is the one that Nick, Lori, and Sheri came up with to meet their needs. Every chart should be uniquely created for the teenager you are attempting to help.

If the teenager embraces this, it will work.

POINT AND LEVEL SYSTEM

Chores at Home

1. Bed made daily
2. Room cleaned once a week
3. Bathroom cleaned twice a week
4. Clothes washed once a week
5. Clothes ironed at night
6. Dishes washed twice a week
7. Table set daily

Points for...

1. Conduct at school, home and church
2. Completing homework daily
3. Completing 15 minutes of (example) clarinet practice...
4. Responsibility for glasses, house key, and band instrument...
5. Completion of daily chores...
6. Completion of weekly chores...
7. Appropriate seating and conduct at church
8. Being responsible for conduct... Being trustworthy with adults...

Point System

DAILY TABLE CHORES DONE ....5 PTS
CLOTHES WASHED (SATURDAY) ....5 PTS
CLOTHES IRONED (NIGHTLY) ....5 PTS
DISHES WASHED (TWICE WEEKLY)......................................20 PTS
BED MADE (DAILY) ....5 PTS
BATHROOM CLEANED (SATURDAY& WEDNESDAY..............10 PTS
HOMEWORK COMPLETED(DAILY)..5 PTS
CLARINET PRACTICE DONE 30 MINUTES (MONDAY THURSDAY)
....5 PTS
GLASSES AND INSTRUMENT SECURED.......................................5 PTS
ATTENDANCE AT CHURCH (WEDNESDAY AND SUNDAY)
....5 PTS

SCHOOL CONDUCT (MONDAY-FRIDAY)...................................15 PTS
TRUSTWORTHINESS AND GOOD ATTITUDE (WEEK – END)
....15 PTS

Scale

90-100 PTS .... ALL PRIVILEGES
80-90 PTS .... LOSS OF WEEK-END PRIVILEGES
70-79............................... LOSS OF ALLOWANCES AND WEEK-END PRIVILEGES
69 and BELOW .... LOSS OF ALL PRIVILEGES FOR ONE WEEK

Rewards

Weekend privileges and allowance must be earned (ball games, movies, spending the night with a friend, or going skating on Fridays, only). Allowance per week... $5.00; Phone time, TV and X Box time Sunday through Thursday for 1 hour, thirty minutes nightly; No phone privileges or TV time until homework is done and clothes are ironed for school.

IF EARNED... Friday nights phone privileges until 11:30 pm;

IF EARNED... Saturday phone privileges until 10:30 pm

Then, Nick and Lori made the decision to let Sheri know that she could always go back to her biological family when and if she wanted to, but after two years, it was their desire for her to live with them. It was when Sheri heard that she had a home with Nick and Lori, that things began to turn around. It was not easy for any of them. Sheri was accustomed to making her own decisions with little structure in her life. Now, Nick and Lori made decisions (like parents of 13 year olds should) for Sheri. Now, Sheri has structure in her life with a Point and Level System that teaches responsibility. But most of all, she has a stable home. She has been reassured by her aunt and uncle that she has a home. She continues to see her mom and siblings, but she also has a permanent place to call home. She can now concentrate on just being a little girl. Her new guardians help her with homework, keep her involved in extracurricular activities, and keep her in a church environment. Give a child love, stability, and structure; then, what you are really giving them is hope. When you give a child peace of mind, they are then able to focus so they can concentrate on learning and growing.

In return, Sheri has been a gift from God to Nick and Lori. It is not what they planned, but they were given an opportunity to do what only a couple like them could do. They provided a Godly home where values, respect, honor, and virtues were displayed. Could it be that the rearing of their own children was the training ground for rearing a child for God? What a privilege it must be to do something special for God. If only what you do for God will last, then what Nick and Lori did for Sheri will go with them into eternity. Only God knows who and what Sheri will grow up to be, but Nick and Lori gave her what a lot of children now-a-days grow up without, a stable home, structure, and love.

Chapter 10

<u>Vacations, A Must for All Families</u>

In all my years of growing up from a baby until I was in my late teens, I never went on a vacation. I remember going on Sunday School picnics on an annual basis. This was a great time for me! My brother, grandma, and I would join our church family and go to various places around our region for a day of frolic, fun, relaxation, and good eating. Getting on a school bus and sometimes even a chartered bus for that trip out of town was awesome! From Mosley Park in Atlanta to Lookout Mountain of Tennessee, we had wonderful days going on the church picnic. The only real experience I had that was like a vacation was as a 12 year old school boy patrol. I earned the right to go on the annual week long adventure to Washington D.C. There, I was able to experience real travel by way of a passenger train, see how the government worked, and be exposed to monuments, buildings and statues that forever changed my life. It was about fifty of us twelve, thirteen, and fourteen year old boys (black and white) with chaperones, and we stayed at a hotel in close proximity to most of these attractions. These were learning and growing experiences I shall never forget, and I credit them with setting me on the path of desiring to travel and see the world.

I say the world; however, the truth is I've only been out of the country (by my choice) three times. I have had my opportunities to go to several countries, but either the timing was not right, the reason was not right, or it just was not the right place. However, name a place in America, and I've probably been there. I was so impressed with Washington D.C. that I persuaded my wife that it was the place we should spend our honeymoon when we were married. Here began my trek through life with my wife that has included vacations on at least an annual basis. To me, a family vacation is imperative even though I never experienced such as a child growing up. I think I turned out just fine, but I am so glad that vacations became one of our family traditions. It is a time for families to get away from the regular rigors and toils of life. It is different and refreshing, and it gives families something to look forward to in the summer months. It is so important to me that I've decided to tell you the process of how we came to where we are now with hopes that you will (if you have not already done so) make vacationing a part of your family's agenda, not just occasionally, but at least once or twice a year.

My honeymoon with my wife was the launching pad for travel. It was a trip that almost did not happen. When we were married, we had no money for a honeymoon. I remember having been given enough money as gifts from friends to take a ride to Atlanta from my hometown of Rome, Georgia, spend the night, and return the next day. On our way to Atlanta, our car broke down. We used that money to get our car fixed and came back home. Little did I know that this was a blessing in disguise. Upon returning to our apartment that night to begin our life together, I promised my wife we would have a honeymoon and many other traveling experiences thereafter. So, we began to do what I suggest every couple should do for the rest of their lives together: Plan for time away from the routine. Plan vacations. Everyone (whether or not you can do it the way you want) deserves to take time off and treat himself to special outings and a little pampering.

We were married in April, but we did not go on our honey moon until June of that year. Why? We could not afford it. You read it right. We waited until we had enough money to make the trip. I will tell you more about that later, but here is the scenario of our honeymoon. First, we had to research what it would cost for gas, accommodations and food to live in Washington D.C. for a week. In 1975, we did not have all the technology to help us; however, we did have maps, telephones, and magazines that could get us all the information we needed. It took us about a week. We made our plans, and when we had saved half of the money needed, we made our reservations. At the time, I had a Volkswagen. We loaded our bicycles on the back so that when we got to the city, we would use them to navigate to the various attractions. The good thing about Washington D.C. was that most of the attractions we wanted to see were free admissions. The Lincoln Memorial, Washington and Jefferson Monuments, Arlington Cemetery, The White House, The Capitol, and the various historical museums were all free of charge. We stayed at a very inexpensive hotel located on the outside of the D.C. area. Each morning, I would drive us into town, park our car, unload the bikes, and off we would go. In those days, you could park and lock the bikes at almost any corner light pole or anywhere there was an unmovable structure. We would pack snack lunches and beverages in back packs. It turned out to be one of the best times of our lives! When we got back in the late afternoon, we would take a shower and relax around the pool. We made friends. Some nights, we'd go for walks. Other nights, we would go out for an evening dinner. No one knew or cared how little we had. In fact, it seemed everyone embraced and appreciated us especially when we met people and shared that we were on our honeymoon.

This went on for the next couple of years. We would carefully plan our next vacation. One of those years we went to Cleveland, Ohio and stayed with relatives. We shared in the expenses of eating, accommodation, and going places to the extent we were allowed. (That has always been a plus for us. We have always had family support outside our immediate family. Get to know your family and establish a relationship with them because you never know who will be there to help you one day.)

About a year after we were married, I graduated from college and joined the United States Air Force. I did my basic training in San Antonio, Texas and my technical training in Biloxi, Mississippi. My first and only tour of duty was at Lowry Air Force Base in Denver, Colorado. Living in Denver, Colorado while being in the military was like being on a three and a half year vacation. I had a great job, the Rocky Mountain's scenery, climate, and beautiful people who had a profound effect on me. I found my home away from home. It was there that my summation of inspiration led me to preach the Gospel of my Lord and Savior, Jesus Christ. Two years after our marriage, we had the first of three children.

Needless to say, with the exception of traveling back home, vacation was otherwise put on the back burner for most of those years. However, when we would go, we remembered the golden rule for us: "Plan." It didn't matter if it was going across country to see our folks for the

Christmas holidays or just going to the mountains to spend a few days, we learned how to plan our trips so that it would be a good experience.

In about four years, we moved back to the South to our hometown, Rome, Georgia. We knew it would be an awesome place to rear our children, plus, my wife wanted to be close to family. Denver had been good to us. I had entered the ministry and we had two of our children born there. Now, we were back home with two small children and another on the way. There were a few years when we did not go on vacation. We were starting a family and family was a blessing of our lives. Nevertheless, it also meant that our income was used to get things in order to provide for these precious little people. We missed our vacations, but we did not grumble or fret for we knew in time it would come up again. That is one hard lesson the military taught me. Learn to live within your means. I want to think I did a fairly good job at that, but I will explain my setback later.

By the time we were taking trips again, our children were ages seven, five, and three. Though they did not fully understand vacations, they certainly enjoyed doing different things. Since they were small, we could also take small vacations once or twice at the beginning and the ending of the summer. My summers were free at this time because I taught school. We would do a long weekend. On Friday, we would go to Atlanta, check into the Marriott Marquis and take advantage of the beautiful city and the things that were offered. For example, we might go to a Braves game Friday Night, Six Flags Theme Park on Saturday, and perhaps stop at White Waters Swimming Park on the way home. Other times, we would go to Stone Mountain, the Zoo, or to other places of interest. Again, the key was planning. Hotels often have discounted rates for various reasons. (You simply have to talk to representatives and barter with them.) The same applies for all the parks and recreational facilities. Remember, small children get in free or at reduced prices. When we stayed at the hotel, we always asked for a top floor. Can you imagine the view for our children? They always slept on the floor for the view, and to count cars, lights, and so on. That was quite an experience for them. Just think, in the late 1970's and early 1980's, we could spend two nights in a plush hotel, go to a ballgame, zoo, and water park and eat well for about $450.00. We had a great time and our children thought they had gone to paradise. My point is that even now you can take weekend getaways to give the family a change of pace, a learning and growing experience, exposure to city life, and just plain fun. Sometimes, I would work a part-time job to have extra money for a couple of weekend getaways in the summer. Again, these were some of the best times of our lives together.

As the family grew, we desired to expose our children to other places. Some of them were excellent for children. Some were just places we had heard of or read about and we wanted to see for ourselves. We were together so the children did not care. Some of our destinations were Niagara Falls, New Orleans, and Manhattan. However, our most often traveled vacation was to our most favorite and popular destination, Orlando, Florida, Walt Disney World, and all the trimmings.

It was and still is our most favorite place to go. However, the first couple of years were more problematic than fun. I simply wasn't ready for all that Orlando and Disney World had to offer. Credit Cards were popular, and I used every one I had. We made our plans; however, I made the mistake of planning with credit cards and believing I could get them paid off within a reasonable period of time. I did not know that the Orlando area or that every hotel and motel franchise was not as safe, clean, and accommodating as others. One vacation, I recall staying at a hotel where we could hear children laughing and playing long past all of our bed times. My wife and I even heard a fight going on next door between a man and wife (we assume husband and wife) that ended up out on the terrace. That was scary. I did not feel comfortable leaving my property in the hotel while I was at the parks. Using credit cards also meant that I would overspend my budget. We would buy things and go places we had not planned. Then, we would come home and worry how we would pay for the debt we had accrued. Another year, our car broke down on us and caused a major repair job. Can you believe I put my wife and three children in the hands of strangers and they safely brought us to our front door without charging us a dime? Days later, I had to drive some 300 miles to the Florida line and tow my car home. Yes, the first couple of years, I could not really enjoy the trip because I was not prepared for uncertain things that can and will happen. Of all my travels, I had never had such a bad experiences, but, the lessons learned were for a lifetime.

For one thing, I got away from planning trips with credit cards. Now, we use them to secure rooms and other incidentals. It is important to always have your money for your trip. It is worth the comfort, cleanliness, and safety. That way, you can enjoy it. My wife and I had an understanding, "When the money is gone, its time to go home." We rededicated ourselves to planning and staying with our plan. I stopped using credit cards. The one thing that ruined my vacation fun was the credit card. I remember coming back up the road wondering and worrying how I was going to pay off all the debt I had made in a week's time. The best vacations are the ones you pay for in advance. You have to save your money and plan for the travel cost, eating, (plus tips) and what parks you're going to visit.

The second lesson learned is to be sure to have good hotel accommodations. You may have to pay a few more dollars, but trust me, it is worth the comfort, cleanliness, and safety. I am proud to tell you that I am a Marriott man, and they have not paid me to endorse them. Decades ago when I was looking for that special place for my family, Marriott was also in the line of choices. In time, I came to see their hotels are a cut above the rest. First, they are plenteous, centrally located, and always clean and up to date. But, most of all, they are safe. Further, they have programs that allow you to earn points by using their credit cards (remember, for purchases you turn right around and pay off) and by staying at their hotels, you earn reward points. Reward points get you all kinds of prizes and free nights at the hotels. All of this plays a very important part in vacationing. Wherever you stay, you want to feel as though you know the people, and the people know you. I find that to be very true with Marriott. That might be the case with other franchises, but again, Marriott is my choice.

As our family continued to grow, five of us ultimately outgrew staying in one room. One thing I could never get used to was my teenagers staying in one room while my wife and I stayed in another, especially if there was not an inside connecting door. That meant that someone could have access to them quicker than I, and I did not like that.

A third point (and this might not be for everyone) is Time Share Villas. I went on vacations for two decades and never considered time share property because I saw them as too expensive and more hype than productive. I would take advantage of staying at them for three nights at a time for a discounted rate and agreeing to see a presentation. I would stay at one villa for three nights for $99.00 per night and go across town and do the same thing all over again. It was a great week. Then, one day I attended a presentation about Villas and was made an offer I thought was more than fair and affordable. It was with Marriott, which also gives me priority to Marriott Hotels when I need one for weekend getaways and business ventures. Moreover, the time share is not only for my wife and me, but it allows us to take our children and grandchildren when they choose to go with us. The point continues to be the same. I am still able to keep my family in a clean, spacious, and safe environment that has the total package. If you are willing to search, barter, and be patient, you can come away with a timeshare that gives you the maximum in vacation.

A few years ago, we decided to take our family to Florida to stay at our 2 bedroom villa, two large bedrooms with two baths with tub, showers, and a spa tub. There is a large common area and a large kitchen. You generally have two balconies, and a pantry (with washer and dryer) and foyer area. Free Wi-Fi access, cable for your three televisions, movies to rent, as well as room service upon request all make this vacation a paradise. The campus is kept clean and security is present everywhere. It is literally a home away from home with all the amenities. We can eat out or prepare full course meals at our villa. A good timeshare property keeps you involved with a lot of fun things on its campus as opposed to going to local attractions. On this particular vacation week, that's exactly what we chose to do. As it turned out, it was only my wife and I and two of our grandchildren. Their ages were six and three years old. We went down with the intent of going to Disney World and perhaps to another major theme park. However, this particular campus had some of everything for everybody, the fitness center for me, the spa department for my wife, a pool haven designed for children, a golf course, lake, excellent restaurants, snack bars, and a campus grocery store. We spent the whole week there and never left the campus. The children never mentioned going to the theme parks because they were having too much fun at the pool with organized play activities (arts and craft, story time, treasure hunts, and other games). Although I was prepared to spend a lot of money, I came back in great shape because this particular campus had all we could imagine to make for a great vacation. A week later, we came home relaxed with happy grandchildren and some extra funds in our pockets. Time share property may not be for you, but it has been tremendous for my family and me, especially since the purchase of it is complete. Now, I can split up my week, use villas other than my home villa, and go anytime of the year. There is an annual maintenance fee, but I can live with that because vacations are important to me.

Keep in mind that vacations mean a time of respite, rest, and relief. For all a family goes through during a year, there ought to be some time away from the routine of work, school, and the other imperatives that make up the routine of life. Once or twice a year, there ought to be a time out from the hustle, bustle, and routine for a break where everyone can relax and just have fun.

Again, we choose Orlando, Florida as our main destination for vacations because it is indeed the vacation capital of the country, maybe even the world. This area has so much to offer and so many things to do. Every child and child at heart ought to visit Disney World and the other Disney theme parks in that area before leaving planet earth. It is not only fun; it is also a learning experience of a variety of subjects. That's right Children are having fun while they learn. It's clean, safe, and you are made to feel special even among thousands of people. Go early, come home, take a break, and go back for an evening session. For the full effect, you might have to do this over a period of days. Yes, the cost is great, but it is worth every penny. And, if you are planning this trip in advance, when you go through the experience, you feel as if it costs you nothing because you prepared in advance, and now you are too busy having fun. However, this is my take on vacations born out of my own experiences. It is up to you to make your own. All I am suggesting to you is that you owe it to yourself and family to have times where you go and treat yourselves like kings and queens. Start with weekend excursions and work your way to the more extended adventures. One thing I am sure of is that you will never regret taking time to simply relax and enjoy your family in other parts of the country or world.., just for the fun of it. I am convinced we are a better family because of it.

Chapter 11

Helping Yourself Before Helping Others

A friend of mine came to me with an issue concerning his son. He had caught him smoking some marijuana in the basement of their home. Naturally, he was upset and livid because he was not going to have his son doing drugs. He had to "nip this in the bud" now and forever. Now, I tried to console and assure him that his son would be ok, and I shared a similar experience I had with my son.

I remember when I was growing up as a teenager in the early 1970's, one of our "rites - of - passage" into adulthood was getting a driver's license. When I got my driver's license and a car, I considered myself grown. For some guys, it was also that first kiss from a special girl, and if you ..., well, those kinds of things made you feel like a man. However, for many of my friends and me, it was that first marijuana cigarette that made me feel like I had crossed the threshold of manhood. I do not know why, but it did. I confessed all this to my friend along with the fact that my uncle had told me of similar situations when he was a teenager in the early 1930's. At that time, it was the first cigarette and first alcoholic drink that was considered crossing over into manhood for him. It is, to some degree, sad that it was how we chose to celebrate that certain time of our lives; however, I personally did not have anyone in my life to tell me any difference. Or, perhaps, I did not listen to them when they did. Is it not so that during our teenage years, all of us did some rather foolish, risky, and even harmful things as our way of saying, "I am grown now"?

So, as the conversation was ending, I noticed that my friend reached into his pocket, pulled out a cigarette and began smoking. Here was one of those life teaching moments where I was able to share with my friend with love and conviction, I asked, "How can you expect your son not to smoke pot (a drug) if his dad smokes cigarettes (a drug)?" Another parent punished his teenager for smoking cigarettes; yet, the teen watched his dad take a couple of alcoholic drinks; every night to sort of "smooth out the rough edges." You do not want your teenage children involved in pre-marital sex; yet, they can follow your entries online and know that you view pornography. Come on. If you are going to help people, you must first be a person of conviction. You cannot say one thing and do another. "Blessed are the pure in heart: for they shall see God" (Matthew **5:8**).

The People's New Testament Commentary explains: "Jesus demands that the heart, the affections, the mind, shall be purified, as the fountain from whence flows the moral and spiritual life. A pure heart begets a pure life; an impure heart, a corrupt life. They shall see God, not with the natural eye, but the spiritual vision, by faith. In the pure heart, the Lord will dwell and His presence will be recognized."

My point is that you cannot preach one thing to your son, mentee, or Sunday School class and do similar detrimental things to your body and mind in the name of "I am grown," or "as long as they do not see me." No, "What is good for the goose is good for the gander." Personally, I think you quench the Spirit when you try to help people deal with issues that you have not yet resolved. A verse of scripture that will set in motion a very important process for all leaders to work on which will ensure that we are equipped to help others is: "Study to shew thyself approved unto God, a workman that needeth not to be ashamed, rightly dividing the word of truth" (2 Timothy 2:15). Now, on the surface, we all see the general call for every Christian to study and prepare themselves to be able to share the Gospel with others to the best of his ability. However, let us look deeper at what that really means. I believe, at the end, you and I will be most challenged to find that God has a great ministry for all of us if we are willing to pay the price.

The Apostle Paul is writing this letter to his favorite son in the ministry, Timothy. Paul is in prison and uncertain as to how long he has to live so he gives Timothy some sound advice and encouragement. Paul loves the Lord, he loves the work of the church, and he loves Timothy. "Thou therefore, my son, be strong in the grace that is in Christ Jesus. And the things that thou hast heard of me among many witnesses, the same commit thou to faithful men, who shall be able to teach others also. Thou therefore endure hardness, as a good soldier of Jesus Christ" (2 Timothy 2:1-3).

In the opening scripture of this chapter, Paul gives three very important points which I will use to begin to make my stance on getting one's self together. First, he tells Timothy, "Be strong in the grace that is in Christ Jesus." That is to say, do not attempt to live the Christian life in your own power. Pray, seek the Lord, read His word, meditate, and then share your gift with others. Second, and most important, he reminds him, "Whatever you've learned from me, whatever good you know about me, make sure you share it with others who you know are sincere about walking with God." As I studied this, I came to realize that for all of us who are sincere about living for God, God himself will put other people in our lives to share with. Yes, we are to be mentors. God will, or God has already put someone in your life for you to mentor them in the ways of God. You don't ask for them, and you don't necessarily pick them, but they are there. Paul did not ask God for Timothy or for any of the other men or women he taught, but God places people in our lives for us to give sound advice and encouragement. The third introduction point is to endure hardness as a good soldier. Doing the will of God will not be easy. Paul knew this, and he wanted Timothy to understand this.

If you look at the Apostle Paul's life, you will know that as well. Taking a stand for Christ is indeed the challenge of your life. However, God will, by His Spirit lead, guide and direct your path. Now, the problem is you cannot take people where you have not gone. You cannot share with people what you do not know. That is why he has said, "Study to show thyself approved unto God." I have to be in the right relationship with God before I can be an example to anyone else. Blues artist, B. B. King, sang a song, "I've got to live the life I sing about in my song." Additionally, I want us to look at how we must handle "the self." First be a diligent self. Study to show thyself approved. The word study (2 Timothy 2:15) initially has nothing to do with books and teachers. Study comes from the Greek word pronounced "spoo-dad'-zo" which means to make an effort to be prompt or earnest:-do (give) diligence, be diligent (forward). Diligence is something done out of love; characterized by steady, earnest, and energetic, painstaking effort. To say this in layman's terms, whatever you do, do it out of love with all your body, soul, and mind. The word study then takes on a whole new meaning.

Notice then, to study means you are your first student. Study to show thyself approved. What God first requires of us is that before we can be any good to anyone else, we must work on self. With all love, steadfastness, and earnestness, I have to study first to get myself together. What kind of pastor am I if I'm trying to encourage others how to live, and my life is a miserable wreck? Moreover, what I've found out is this: God will not bless me to be of any help to others (in other words he will not anoint me, possess me, or use me) until I have fully surrendered myself to him. Therefore, it is not enough for us to just study the word and impart knowledge to others. That is good. You have to do that, but, I know from experience that your efforts to move people for Christ is in vain if the Christ you talk about is not dwelling, with authority and power in you.

Secondly, the self must be "approved unto God." I believe that one of the biggest problems facing man is learning to please God and not himself and those around him. Paul makes this perfectly clear when he points out that we all have two selves. "This I say then, Walk in the Spirit, and ye shall not fulfill the lust of the flesh. For the flesh lusteth against the Spirit, and the Spirit against the flesh: and these are contrary the one to the other: so that ye cannot do the things that ye would" (Galatians *5:16-17).* That is a great challenge for us. It is an internal battle to deny the flesh in order for the spirit man to rule our life. "Then said Jesus unto his disciples, If any man will come after me, let him deny himself, and take up his cross, and follow me" (Matthew 16:24). When you come to Christ, he saves you, he begins to sanctify and cleanse you and he fills you with His spirit. But, the one thing He asks of us is to deny the flesh, the selfish self, the self-centered self, and let His spirit take control over the body, soul, and mind. That's what "self approved unto God" means. When God's spirit controls your spirit, He leads you to a strong prayer life, a strong devotional life, and a call to service, and ministry. Then, you begin to experience life and life more abundantly. Now, that does not mean you are going to necessarily be rich and that everything goes your way. However, it does mean that whatever you go through or whatever you are up against, God is with you and you have the victory of life.

Let me sum up this second point by telling you the story of the pastor, preacher, and hymnologist, Reverend Dr. Charles Tindley. He was born July 7, 1851 in Berlin, Maryland. Born to slave parents and separated from them when only fives years of age, Tindley was a most remarkable individual. He learned to read and write on his own by the time he was 17. He attended night school, completed seminary training through correspondence, and was ordained to the Methodist ministry. While attending evening school, young Tindley supported himself as the janitor of the Calvary Methodist Episcopal Church in Philadelphia in 1902. Tindley was later called to pastor this prestigious church where he had once been the janitor. The Calvary Methodist Church prospered greatly under his leadership. Eventually, several larger sanctuaries had to be built to accommodate the crowds of all races that came to hear this humble preacher. In 1924, in spite of Tindley's protest, the new church building was renamed the Tindley Temple Methodist Church. Under his leadership, the church grew from 130 to a multiracial congregation of 10,000. Tindley was the first hymn writer to have a hymn copyrighted. He never intended for his songs to be sung in formal worship services but rather on informal occasions. He published a hymn collection in 1916, entitled *New Songs of Paradise.* He put God first and was richly rewarded for it. Here was a man who was diligent, disciplined, and ultimately a disciple of our Lord and Savior, Jesus Christ, which leads to my third and final point.

Finally, when you become truly disciplined, you are on your way to becoming a disciple of whatever it is you have studied. In other words, you are becoming the disciple, the steward, the self that God intends you to be. You are not ashamed of who you are, or whose you are. Because of your walk with God, now you can rightly divide the word. Rightly dividing means cutting straight and can be applied to many different tasks: plowing a straight furrow, cutting a straight board, sewing a straight seam, and being a powerful influence to those around you. The Bible becomes your tool for building, measuring, and repairing God's people. In other words, God gives us at least one gift to reach others and build on the kingdom of God. "As every man hath received the gift, even so minister the same one to another, as good stewards of the manifold grace of God" (1 Peter 4:10). I'm reminded of what Paul finally told Timothy, "Stir up Your Gift." It is in you. Stir it up.

Gospel singer, Yolanda Adams, said, "When you love what you are doing, it is not work. When you love what you do, you never grow tired of doing it. When you love what you do, it energizes you, it gives you joy, and it brings peace". "And the peace of God, which passeth all understanding, shall keep your hearts and minds through Christ Jesus. Finally, Brethren, whatsoever things are true, whatsoever things are honest, whatsoever things are just, whatsoever things are pure, whatsoever things are lovely, whatsoever things are of good report; if there be any virtue, and if there be any praise, think on these things. Those things, which ye have both learned, and received, and heard, and seen in me, do: and the God of peace shall be with you" (Philippians 4:7-9).

Kirk Franklin, after receiving his third Stellar Award for his Gospel work, told the story about the playful boy who was second string on a high school football team. He seemed to never take the game seriously, always playing and clowning around. Yet, as it would be, a first string player got hurt, and the boy went into the game and literally took the game over. He scored touchdowns, intercepted the ball from the opposing team, and made tackles. He literally won the game for his team. When he was asked what had come over him, his response was, "My father was blind most of my life and he died yesterday. Today was the first day my father got to see me play. I wanted to do well because I knew my father was watching me". This should be our goal: We must do and be our best so that we can help others to be their best because our Heavenly Father is watching us.

In conclusion, I want to encourage you that I believe that our children and young people will have a bright future. All they need is our guidance and support. Therefore, I challenge you to never pass up an opportunity to help yourself. When we as parents, tutors, mentors, and leaders demonstrate high moral character it will be embraced by our children. Love what you do and show it; enthusiasm moves mountains. Prayerfully, change directions to meet changing times. If you stand still, you will begin a progressive decline in your ability to help others. Look and act your best. As a follower of Christ, project a very special image. Always try to keep one realistic goal in front of you when it comes to ministering to children. Take risks and do not be afraid to make mistakes. Just remember to learn and grow from your experiences. Be confident and believe in yourself; That is to say, be positive because negativism destroys enthusiasm, creativity, and achievement. Enjoy, have fun, and be happy with the task that is before you. Listen to your intuitive self and when you feel the need, take time to nurture yourself. Remember, if you think you can or can not, you are right. Now, if you have taken the time to read this book, I want you to know that I believe that your call and purpose is to strive to make a difference in a child's life. We can do all things through Christ who strengthens us. Join me in this journey of making a difference in a child's life.

References

The Holy Bible: New Revised Standard Version. 1996, 6989 (Genesis 2:24). Nashville: Thomas Nelson.

13th Gen: Abort, Retry, and Ignore, Fail? by Neil Howe and Bill Strauss. Vintage Books, Random House, Inc. New York, New, 1993, Pg.12 Page 16,17

lPfeiffer, C. F. (1962). The Wycliffe Bible commentary : Old Testament (Proverbs 13:24). Chicago: MoodyPress.

Nurturing God's Way, Parenting Program for Christian Families, Sue Laney and Nancy McClure, Second Edition, copyright 2005, Family Developyment Resources, Inc.

United Way of America and the Enterprise Foundations. Source: Partnerships for Success: A MentoringProgram Manual, 1990).

Merriam-Webster Dictionary, http://aolsvc.merriam-webster.aol.com/homeaol.htm

Palo Alto Medical Foundation: www.pamf.org/teen/health/diseases/obesity.html

Online: ABC, Good Morning America, February 9, 2010, Robin Roberts interviews Michelle Obama, reported by Lee Ferran.

How to Begin a Children's Ministry I eHow.com htt-o://www.ehow.com/how 2072835 beQin-childrensministry.html#ixzz2LSTMBoyZ

Psychological Disorders of Children, A Behavioral Approach to Theory, Research, and Therapy, Second Edition, by Alan 0. Ross, McGraw-Hill Book Company, 1980

Printed by Libri Plureos GmbH in Hamburg, Germany